the idea book
for scrapbooking

Nona's Tea Party

Nona O'Brian Cathcart - on the right - born approximately
1882 - sister of Jeffrey Louis Nelp's paternal grandmother
Marjorie O'Brian Nelp

THE IDEA BOOK FOR SCRAPBOOKING
by TweetyJill Publications

ISBN 1-891898-02-7 Library of Congress, Catalog Card Number 98-96812

Copyright© 1999 by TweetyJill Publications, Inc. All rights reserved
First published in the United States by TweetyJill Publications, Sarasota, Florida.
The material in this book is intended for personal use only. No part of this publication may be reproduced, transmitted
or stored in any form or by any means, electronic or mechanical, without prior written permission from the publisher.

This book was produced by TweetyJill Publications, Inc.
PMB 412, 5824 Bee Ridge Road, Sarasota, Florida 34233 ❂ 1-800-595-5497

Book Design Carol King ❂ **Writers** Jill Haglund, Yvonne Perez, Lindsay Haglund ❂ **Editors** Rob Haglund,
Meg Raben ❂ **Poetry** Linda Jones, Treasured Reflections ❂ **Photography** Herb Booth Studio, Inc., Herb Booth;
Heintz-Wassoon Photography, Michael Heintz; Christopher Darling Photography, Christopher Darling
❂ **Photo Stylists** Dale Clancy, Rachel North, Christine Diguisetti ❂ **Scrapbook Artists** Jill Haglund,
Karen Wiessner, Trecia Northrup, Lori Pieper, Sharon Kropp, Norma Manak, Amy Nelp, Diane Wieder, Cindi Byers,
Marieda Sawyer, Alison Nunley, Shannon Torgerson, Debbie Miles, Shari Valencic-Ursel, Lindsay Ostrom, Vicki Breslin,
Vicki Garner, MarJean Boyter, Marjorie Klein, Jane Engebretson, Jody Homan, Jeanne Motley and Lynette Clock

BOOK COVER CREDITS
Photography by Herb Booth; design by Rob Haglund and Carol King. Rubber stamps:
Eiffel Tower and Big Ben by All Night Media®; Luggage Tag and Suitcase by Judi-Kins®.

Printed in China

You finally finagle a way to work on your album a few hours; husband away, children napping; at last, time to devote to scrapbooking. Then it happens—a big white scrapbook page is staring back at you! "Where do I start?" you say," I finally get some time to create a page and I am at a loss for ideas! " Well, never again—now that you have **The Idea Book For Scrapbooking** in your hands.

I want to thank the dozens of women who have given their time, talent and "labor of love" to create this beautiful compilation of unique scrapbooking styles. Pages poured into our office from all across the country and I came to feel that each new arrival was like opening a special present. I hope this book will pass that excitement and creative passion on to you as well.

Each of us has an independent style, but we all improve with shared ideas and techniques. Once you have duplicated a layout with your very own photographs, it becomes your page!

Scrapbookers love paper products, so the book really features paper crafting. Paper is an easy and economical way to design your scrapbook. Templates and scissors are the only creative tools you really need to add.

Rubber stamping is another love of scrapbookers and we used them extensively in the collages as well as the Family Heritage, Music, Travel Abroad and Beach chapters. If you have a variety of a dozen classic rubber stamp images (e.g., as leaves, flowers, shells, sayings, frames, hearts, and design elements or icons), you can create a whole album. I hope you let your imagination run wild layering different papers, inks and stamps. The collages within the pages will help get your creative juices flowing.

Linda Jones has very graciously shared her treasured God-given poetry with us. She has a gift for saying exactly what I feel about my children, family and other loved ones. I encourage you to contact Treasured Reflections; use her charming poems, printed on acid-free paper, for "title pages" in your album.

Don't forget to add meaning to your scrapbook with journaling, too. Your explanations of the events surrounding your pictures add a personal touch to your memories. I hope you enjoy creating new pages with the ideas to follow. Now let's start scrapbooking!

Creatively Yours,

Jill

Jill Haglund
President of TweetyJill Publications

Table of Contents
Twenty Themed Chapters

Je t'aime
Mukuràréta i love

CORRESPONDENZ-KARTE

Besty Oliva Custer with
child, Marian, age, 3mo. and
age 4yrs.
Betsy's
father is
also pictured
George Knowden.
Betsy's husband was killed
in civil war in 1864 when
Marian was 3yr. His name was John.

Memories
are like Flowers that God Plants
in our Hearts, that Bloom and
Fill our Lives with Love as the

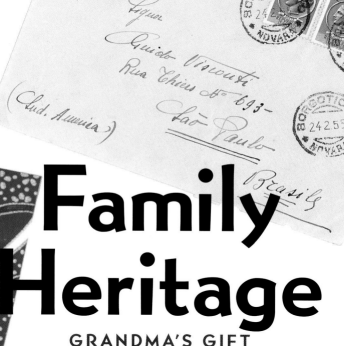

Family Heritage

GRANDMA'S GIFT

A grandma is made up of wonderful things
Lovely and glowing—such treasures she brings
With a sweet, gentle spirit she knows just the way
To spread joy and laughter and brighten each day...

When her family needs her, Grandma's always there
To lend a hand or ease a pain that someone has to bear
She's gained alot of wisdom from all that she's been through
And she'll give all she has to make one small dream come true.

Everything's more special when she plays a part
From secrets to surprises, she's sure to warm your heart
Through the years so gracefully her legacy will flourish
To all whose lives she's touched so well...a gift of love to cherish!

Excerpts from "Grandma's Gift," a poem by Linda Jones, Treasured Reflections.
Copyright 1996. All rights reserved.

Opposite: Album page by Exposures. Paper and photo corners by Canson. Aspen leaf rubber
stamp by Northwoods. Word stamp by Hampton Art Stamps. Botanical rubber
stamp by Personal Stamp Exchange. Mulberry paper by Papers by Catherine.

5

WE'RE IN THE ARMY

Ft. Bragg, CA.

NOW

River Park

Relaxing By the Lake...

The Sweet Peiper Children

All in the FAMILY

Captain Louis Nelp

WWII

PILOT TRAINING

1	2	3
4	5	6
7	8	9

TIP: Today's military training photos are part of tomorrow's family heritage collection.

TIP: A worthwhile investment is Pebbles Tracer templates. You can create oodles of different letter styles and feed your creativity for years to come.

1 Paper, photo corners and die cuts by Canson. An embossing pen was used to put details on die cut shapes —then embossed with gold embossing powder by Ranger.

2 Torn paper mats created with an Art Deckle ruler. Classic colored paper by Canson. Banners are a perfect way to feature a family name.

3 Paper, photo corners and die cut shapes by Canson. Designer Sticker Letters by Déjà Views.

4 Military die cut shapes sold by Cut-It-Up. You can find the lettering in "LMNOP...More Creative Letters With Lindsay," by Lindsay Ostrom.

5 Adhesive-backed die cuts, photo corners and paper by Canson. Nautilus shell and scallop rubber stamp images by Rubber Stampede. Sand dollar image and masterpiece quotation by Personal Stamp Exchange. All have been embossed with gold embossing powder by Ranger.

6 Paper and photo corners by Canson. Oak leaf stamp and friendship stamp by Personal Stamp Exchange. Leafy Limb stamp by Posh Impressions. Zig Opaque Gold Writer used for lettering. Frame created with trimmer by Fiskars.

7 Paper by Geographics. Déjà Views template used to crop pictures. Zig Opaque Writer used for lettering.

8 Paper and photo corners by Canson. Lettering created with Zig Opaque Writer. WWII has been traced and cut from paper by Canson using a lettering template by Déjà Views.

9 "Pilot Training" lettering hand cut. Camouflage paper by Frances Meyer, Inc. Letters traced with a Marvy Uchida gel roller.

 10 "Nelp Kids" was hand-lettered with Zig pens. "Jeff" was created using Pebbles Tracer. **11** Patterned paper by D.J. Inkers, designed by Dianne J. Hook. Borders created by tracing and cutting a Déjà Views ruler design on Canson paper. Center die cut by Ellison. Acid-free doily by The Ehlers Company, Incorporated Imports. Mats made with a template by Déjà Views and a Punchline craft punch by McGill. **12** Canson paper and gold photo corners. Fern stamped image by Hero Arts; paper trimmed with Family Treasures Jumbo Series Wave Scissor. On second page, all frames and paper by Canson. Lettering created with a Zig Opaque Writer. Daisy punches by Marvy Uchida. Some daisies are folded in half, others are layered in pairs or simply used alone.

TIP: Rubber stamp images give character to a family history book.

13 Canson paper and photo corners. Stampington & Co. music rubber stamp. Paper mats torn with an Art Deckle ruler. Mat edges embossed with gold embossing powder by Ranger. **14** Paper and photo corners by Canson. Braided paper border created with Déjà Views Wave Ruler. Heart shapes created with Marvy Uchida's punches.

13
14

TIP: Use the stainless steel Art Deckle ruler and paper by Canson to make torn mats for your family heritage photographs.

15 Magnolia rubber stamp and large ivy by Personal Stamp Exchange. Gold embossing powder and black Archival Ink by Ranger. All paper and photo corners by Canson. **16** First page—acorn rubber stamp by Personal Stamp Exchange and small maple leaf by Hero Arts Rubber Stamps. Paper and photo corners by Canson. Wave Jumbo Series Scissors by Family Treasures. Second page—large ivy rubber stamp by Personal Stamp Exchange and small leaf rubber stamp by Northwoods. Gold embossing powder and Sepia Archival Ink by Ranger. Opaque gold pen by Zig.

TIP: Black scrapbook pages can be very striking, and truly enhance color as well as historical photos.

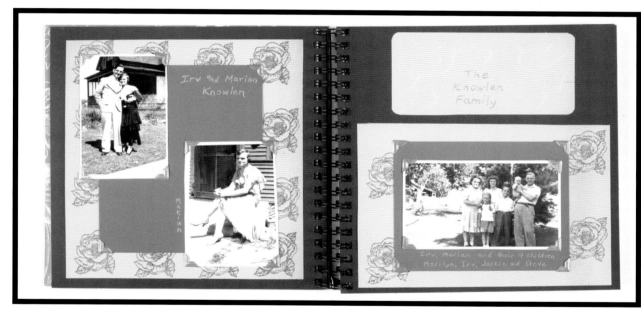

17 A timeless and classic look. Canson paper was torn using an Art Deckle ruler. Posh Impressions' Leafy Limb rubber stamp embossed with gold powder. A Judi-Kins spiral rubber stamp was embossed with green powder on blue paper by Canson, the second page has Hero Arts sunflower rubber stamp embossed with gold powder by Ranger. Family Treasures' Mini Antique Elegance scissors used to cut the border and mat. Gold photo corners by Canson. **18** Paper and photo corners by Canson. Magnolia rubber stamp by Personal Stamp Exchange. Lettering created with Zig Opaque Writer.

17

18

19 Paper by Canson. Family Treasures' Slot Corner punch. **20** Paper by Canson. Lace paper by Paper Pizazz from Hot Off the Press (hereinafter referred to as H.O.T.P.). Writing created with Zig Memory Series Colored Pencils. **21** Paper and photo corners by Canson. Zig Opaque Gold Writer. Hand-cut lamb shape. **22** Paper and photo corners by Canson. Ivy paper by Keeping Memories Alive. Photo tinting done with the Marshall's Photo Tinting Kit.

23 Paper and photo corners by Canson. All rubber stamps by Inkadinkado. **24** Patterned paper by Creative Card. Banner template by Provo Craft. Banner lettering created with pens by Zig. Paper cuts made with Fiskars Deckle and Arabian Paper Edgers. Stickers by Mrs. Grossman. Oval template by Déjà Views used to crop photo. **25** Paper and photo corners by Canson. Lace paper by Paper Pizazz from H.O.T.P. Photos cropped with Déjà Views template. Acid-free pens by Zig. Banner cut with Provo Craft template. **26** Paper by Canson. Majestic Paper Edgers by Fiskars used to crop mat. Ivy frame by Mara-mi. Banner template by Provo Craft.

23	24
25	26

TIP: Make sure to include childhood friends, teenage memories and favorite teachers in your heritage album.

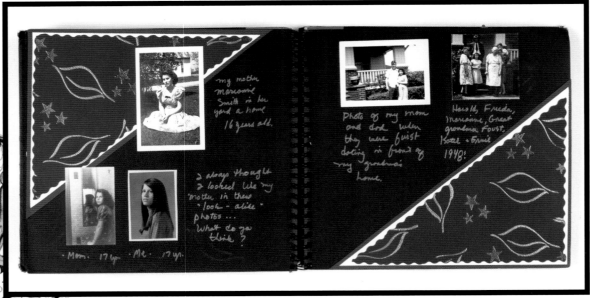

27 Photo corner stamps by Straightforward Stamps. Oak Leaf rubber stamp by Personal Stamp Exchange. Paper by Canson. Lettering done with Opaque Gold Writer by Zig. Photos were matted on black paper for a classic look. Gold photo corners by Canson. Majestic Paper Edgers by Fiskars were used for layered corner borders. Maple and Oak Leaf rubber stamps by Personal Stamp Exchange. Leafy Limb stamp by Posh Impressions. Aspen Leaf rubber stamp by Northwoods Rubber Stamps. All images were embossed with Ranger's Verdigris embossing powder. Lettering created with Zig Opaque Writer. **28** Paper and album by Canson. Brushed leaf by Denami Designs. Star trio rubber stamp by Rubber Stampede. Silver and copper embossing powder by Ranger. Lettering by Zig Opaque Gold Writer. Family Treasures Wave Jumbo Series Scissors.

27
28

29 Two shades of Crow's Feet paper by MPR's Paperbilities III. Photos matted on Canson paper. Lettering done with acid-free pens by Zig. **30** Canson paper, die cuts and photo corners make a timeless looking page. **31** Paper, album and die cuts by Canson. Photo corner designs created with Corner Lace Punches by Family Treasures. Lettering achieved with an Opaque Gold Writer by Zig.

29 30
31

32 Paper and photo corners by Canson. Leafy Limb rubber stamp by Posh Impressions. Brushed Leaf rubber stamp by Denami Design. **33** Canson paper and photo corners. Torn frames created with an Art Deckle ruler and embossed with gold embossing powder by Ranger. Queen Anne's Lace rubber stamp by Wildlife Enterprises. Words & Memories Series stamps by TweetyJill Publications.

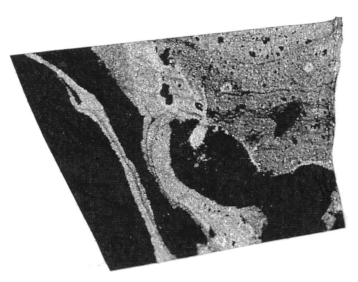

32

33

TIP: Photo corners are small, right-angle photo mounts. They come in a variety of colors. These are the same corners your great grandma probably used in her scrapbooks; except then, she could get them only in black. First, place them on the corners of a trimmed photo; then, moisten the back and adhere to your paper (or even directly to your scrapbook page). Photo corners are just another way of displaying snapshots. One great feature of photo corners is they do not require permanent bonding of a photograph to a page. This is an especially good way to mount old family photographs, since you may want to remove them at a later date, to photocopy for additional albums for family members.

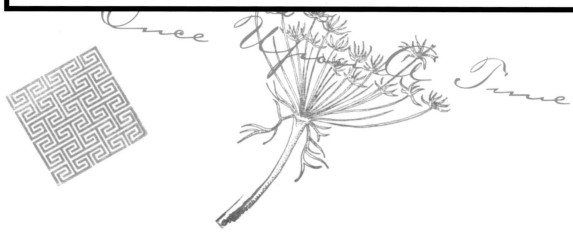

Family

FOREVER A FAMILY

God took a man, searched far and wide, and led him to a wife
Someone to share his hopes and dreams—together build a life
He saw that they were happy, and knew that it was good
So He blessed them with some miracles— the greatest way He could.

He created little angels to entrust unto their care
Making each one very specially, to more fully bind the pair
Together they would make a home, where they would all belong
To laugh and cry and grow and love— together they'd be strong...

The family grew together, their lives so well entwined
And each day shared between them left some memories behind
Of smiles and surprises and many dreams-come-true
In good times and in bad times, they helped each other through...

So as your angels grow, remember that each day
Is filled with fleeting memories that somehow find a way
Of nestling deep within your heart to treasure and hold fast
The precious family times that all too soon become the past.

Excerpts from "Forever A Family," a poem by Linda A. Jones, Treasured Reflections.
Copyright 1997. All rights reserved.

Opposite: Hand cut from Canson papers. Marvy Uchida Brites Series gel rollers were used for embellishments.

1	2	3
4	5	6
7	8	9

TIP: Don't forget to take black-and-white photographs every now and then.

TIP: Start a friend scrapbooking by giving her "The Complete Guide To Scrapbooking" as a gift. She'll be hooked after reading it!

1 A Puzzlemate template by Quick Cuts created this layout. Patterned paper by Paper Patch . Stitches on template shapes made with Marvy Brites Series gel rollers.

2 Paper, die cuts and border designs by Canson. Photo corners were made from Canson self-adhesive paper, then layered.

3 Mats are trimmed with Marvy Uchida's Corner Rounder. Sunset, clouds, fence and grass were created with Canson paper.

4 "Jake" was created with Pebbles Tracer template. The layout of the domino was made with a Fiskars trimmer and a Circle Cutter. Paper by Canson.

5 Have fun designing your own patchwork quilt with punched shapes and penned "stitches." Punches by Marvy Uchida, Family Treasures and McGill.

6 Lettering is hand-cut. Paper by Wubie Print. You don't have to crop any photos if you don't want to, and here a is a prime example!

7 Die cuts and photo corners by Canson. Accu-Cut Scrapbook font die cut letters. Mat stamped with a Family Memories Series rubber stamp by TweetyJill Publications.

8 Circular mats cut with Fiskars Celestial Paper Edgers. Circle Cutter by Fiskars used on photos. Top photo trimmed and matted with Summit Corner Edgers. Bottom border created with a ruler by Déjà Views. Grass is hand cut.

9 All paper by Canson. Border shapes and corner edges are self-adhesive die cut paper shapes by Canson. Lettering created with pens by Zig.

TIP: Create little pieces of artwork for your scrapbook page by punching out shapes and designing them to work together!

21

Sisters are the flowers in the garden of life!

babes & bows

BIG SISTER

I have a big sister;
She's taller and older;
On tiptoe I only
Reach up to her shoulder;
But I have a secret
That I haven't told her
(It's time to grow faster
Until I grow past her.)

I watch what she's eating;
I watch what she's drinking,
I don't let her notice
Or see what I'm thinking,
But each time that she
Takes a bite, I take two;
And that way the only
Eats half what I do.

I have a big sister;
She's taller and older;
On tiptoe I only
Reach up to her shoulder;
But I have a secret
That I haven't told her
(The way I will beat her
Is just to outeat her!)

Sarah and Tessie

Sisters and Best Friends

"Sarah & Jessica romping around with Danielle!" October, 1995

Sarah holding Jessica after a bath. Summer, 1997

10 This page layout uses Paper Patch Paper and has Provo Craft Designer Sticky Die Cut flowers and leaves. Photos are matted and trimmed with Uchida's Corner Rounder. **11** Bow is hand-cut from Design Originals "Scrap Happy" paper, and embellished with a red pen by Zig. Border template is by Pebbles. Letters are Déjà Views' Designer Letters. This is an easy, eye-pleasing way to balance a composition of cut and matted oval-shaped snapshots. Try it with family heritage photographs, too! **12** The heart-shaped Puzzlemate Template design by Quick Cuts makes any photo grouping special. A Fiskars Arabian Paper Edger gave the heart-shaped white mat a Victorian flair. **13** Acid-free doilies by Ehlers Company, Inc., Imports. Stickers by Mrs. Grossman's. Fiskars Paper Edgers used to trim mats.

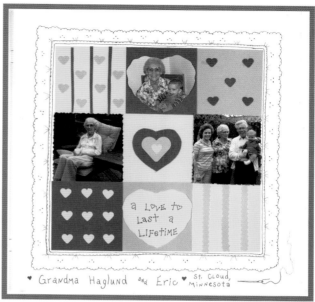

TIP:
Go to your local fine art store to find the full selection of Canson acid-free colored papers.

14 Karen created this page of Sarah and her dad using Family Treasures' paper punches. Throughout the scrapbook she uses the words from the song "Butterfly Kisses." This album will be given to Sarah, by her dad, on her wedding day. 15 Lace border was a hand-drawn labor of love for Grandma Haglund by her granddaughter Karen. Heart-punched shapes used on this quilt page are made with Marvy Uchida Punches. 16/17 Fiskars Paper Edgers trimmed the heart shapes. The "Grandparents" cut-out was made using Pebbles Tracers. Border created with a Marvy Uchida heart punch. This page looks striking because of the beautiful Canson colors.

| 14 | 15 |
| 16 | 17 |

Sisters & Brothers

Sisters

 18 "My brother, my friend" photo mounted on paper by Geographics. Mat made with an Art Deckle ruler. All other paper is by Canson.   **19** Designer Sticky Letters by Déjà Views. Side border is cut with Mammoth Accents Scissors by Paper Adventures. Design created with a Quick Cuts Puzzlemate Template.   **20** Watermelon created with checked paper by Paper Patch. Flowers and leaves were all hand-made. Bird sticker by Mrs. Grossman's. Heart punch by Marvey Uchida.   **21** Simple and artistic! Colored strips of paper make easy, clean-looking borders. Spot lettering template by The C-Thru Ruler Company.

TIP: Expand your creativity; try enhancing your scrapbook pages with embossed rubber-stamped designs. The artwork is already done—just stamp it!

22 "Wieder Kids" page designed with MPR and Associates' Paperbilities III papers. Pebbles Tracer template used for lettering. Smaller white lettering created with Zig Opaque Writer. 12" by 12" background paper by MPR Associates Paperbilities III. **23** Paper by Canson. Accu-Cut die cuts make a great "Family Tree." **24** Best of Friends and Aspen Leaf rubber stamps by Personal Stamp Exchange. Sunflower stamp by Portfolio. Copper embossing powders by Ranger. Photo matted with photo corners by Canson. Mats trimmed with a Fiskars Deckle Paper Edger. Mat corners created with a Fiskars Summit Corner Edger. **25** This page is made entirely of Hallmark scrapbooking products. The Hallmark line includes creative and unique photo corners, papers, stickers, die cuts, and borders.

22	23
24	25

TIP: Say what is in your heart, and touch someone else's with poetry.

Marigold

If all else fails
Hug your Teddy

IJKL
Friends

Friends are kindred spirits, loving unconditionally, always ready with a kind ear and the strength to help you face whatever life brings. They laugh together, lean on one another and defend each other. Childhood friendships evolve so beautifully and seamlessly from sharing toys to clothes to hopes and dreams. Youth possesses uninhibited, limitless possibilities and maturity is built with hurts and triumphs through the years. Growing up means making friends and learning what it means to be a good one.

What a joy it is to find a snapshot of your best friend standing next to the moving van the day she arrived next door, and place it next to the newspaper clipping of her latest achievement. Friendship transcends time and distance. With friends, you can always be yourself and they will love you anyway. They speak heart to heart and soul to soul. Friends are priceless jewels in our crowns; treasures that make our lives complete.

TIP: Nothing bonds friends like Scrapbooking together. You get to share stories, photos, laughter, tears, memories and a piece of your heart.

TIP: Punch flower shape first. Next, layer a contrasting color spiral on top of the flower or punch a spiral into the flower. Then glue to another paper color.

A smile is a smile in any language.

1	2	3
4	5	6
7	8	9

TIP: Never cut original old photos; make copies to crop. Always label at least who, what, where and when!

1&2 Certain snapshots allow themselves to be cut into large letters. First make your own templates of the letters you need and lay over the photo, then adjust for positioning. You may be able to make small changes in the letter size or design to make it fit. Now mount your "letter photo" onto another sheet of paper and trim leaving a small margin of color.

3 Paper by Canson, trimmed with Pinking Paper Edgers by Fiskars. Déjà Views template used to crop photos. "Friends" made with Pebbles Funky Tracer and Zig Opaque Writers.

4 Patterned paper by Design Originals. Pebbles Tracer was used to do the creative lettering. Déjà Views Mix n' Mat template was used for photo mats and page corners.

5 Friendship is special in any language. Barry and Lynn, our Chinese friends, hold a special place in our hearts, so we all created a page together combining English and Chinese languages and heartfelt messages. Uchida punches and Accu-Cut heart die cuts.

6 All paper by Canson. Ivy brass embossing template by Lasting Impressions. Corner Punch by Family Treasures. Green and black plaid paper by Wubie Print.

7 For "New Kid on the Block," the blocks were created with the diamond-shaped geometric template from Déjà Views. Heart-shaped punches by Marvy Uchida.

8 Hand cut grass for a lower border and add letters so they peek thru the blades. This page works well for sports, graden, camping, picnic, park or playground snapshots.

9 Mrs. Grossman's stickers create a picnic for a bottom border design. Page by Vicki Breslin.

TIP: If one of your acid-free markers gets tainted by another color when doodling or drawing borders, roll the tip across a wet paper towel to clean.

TIP: You can use colored pencils to add color to your stamped image. Try Zig's Memory Series Pencils.

TIP: When you use dye-based inks for stamping, you can watercolor and use markers on the image without the colors bleeding.

What an awesome pet!

"Yikes! He's kissing me!"

My little brother liked him, too!

Spike the iguaNa

rover
spot
spud
jaws

Puppy's Journal

Pets

THERE MUST BE DOGS IN HEAVEN

There must be dogs in heaven—of this I'm pretty sure
For there's no other creature with a heart so big and pure
They are a treasure sent from God— a gift as fine as gold
And once you get to know one, you'll see true character unfold.

Be cautious when you meet one 'cause once you let her stay
She'll become just like your family and steal your heart away
She'll love you 'til forever— no matter what you do
You'll always be her master— she'll be faithful through and through...

She'll play with you 'til time stands still and never seem to tire
Do all her little tricks for you—true friendship she'll inspire
She'll develop funny habits that will fill your heart with laughter
And the memories shared together, you will hold forever after...

I think God made dogs specially to help us as we live
And make our days much brighter with the happiness they give
And I know that God has set aside in heaven special places
With cool, green grass; fresh, clear water; and miles of open spaces.

It's here that God will hold them where they'll run and rest and play
As they wait there for their masters to unite again someday
So if that special friend of yours and you should ever part
Know she'll wait for you in heaven like she did right from the start.

Excerpts from "There Must Be Dogs In Heaven," a poem by Linda A. Jones, Treasured Reflections.
Copyright 1994. All rights reserved.

TIP: Tear mats for your photo using the Art Deckle ruler. Then, mount the snapshots in photo corners for a finished look!

TIP: Only create those extra-special pages "once in a while." You want to get your albums done in this lifetime! But you can "wow" them every now and then.

1 Sticker letters by K & Company. Gold embossing was done before trimming with a Fiskars Rotary Cutter (wave blade). Punched shapes made with Family Treasures' flower punches.

2 Embossed and chalk paw prints done with a brass stencil, stylus and green chalk. All paper and die cuts by Canson.

3 Lettering done with Zig pens. Photo corners made with adhesive-backed Canson paper. Photos cropped with Fiskars trimmer.

4 This is a special page for Luke's memory book. Oval template by Déjà Views. Paper by Canson. Lettering done with Zig pens.

5 Use the Déjà Views Mix n' Mat template to crop and make frames for photographs. Mix and match them; they all work together! Lettering done with white Zig Opaque Writer.

6 Now isn't this a fun page for your little insect lovers? We definitely rate this with four stars for labor intensive and for awesome! Pebbles Tracers created the lettering.

7 Dog and paws paper shapes by Canson. Photo and mat cut with a Fiskars Circle Cutter. Border and square mat created with a Déjà Views ruler.

8/9 Hannah lives in Alaska and is a dog musher. Her coach, Ron Kilian, shot these award-winning photographs. "Dog sledding" is written with a wide tip Opaque Writer by Zig. Crisp snowflakes by Provo Craft. Border was designed with a Déjà Views ruler. All paper is from Canson.

TIP: Choose some of your favorite nature (or scenery) snapshots and make a special page to feature them for memories sake. But, make sure you record when and where you took them.

TIP: The templates by Mix 'n Mat are especially designed to work with each other. Use the templates with classic paper colors. Be daring with bold, or create a page in soft pastel colors.

33

10 11
12 13

10 Lettering done with a Pebbles Tracer. Paws by Frances Meyers. Mouse die cut and paper by Canson. **11** Lettering created with Pebbles Tracer and D.J. Inkers Paper by Dianne J. Hook. Embossed images made with a template from Déjà Views. Background paper by Paper Patch. Lettering was done with a white Zig Opaque Writer. **12** All patterned paper by Paper Patch. Bone was hand-cut. Paw print die cut by Canson. Circular photo and mat cut with a Fiskars Circle Cutter. Lettering was done using a Pebbles Tracer. **13** Sarah and Lindsay spoil Pete with food, hugs, tail braiding and lots of love! The rope was created with Fiskars Paper Edgers and detailed with pen. The horseshoes were embossed first from a template and then traced with pen. The title looks like a wooden sign. All paper by Canson.

paper! You won't have to search for a particular sticker or that perfect design. These pages can be made by anybody with cool papers.

14 Dog print paper by Design Originals. Stickers by Frances Meyer. Lettering created with a Pebbles Tracer and paper by Canson. Trim and mat photos with a Marvy Uchida Corner Rounder. **15** Bunny die cuts by Accu-Cut. Paper by Canson. Photo double-matted and trimmed with a Fiskars trimmer. **16** Paw prints paper by Paper Patch. Designer Letters by Déjà Views. Photos trimmed and matted with a trimmer. **17** Denim paper by Frances Meyers, Inc. Corrugated and burlap papers by Paper Pizazz by H.O.T.P. Sheriff's badge, fence and cactus by Provo Craft. Horse die cut by Ellison.

14	15
16	17

18 19
20

18 Here is a collage of fun dog times. Prints leading up to doghouse and on the borders were made with a Hero Arts rubber stamp. Template used for cropping by Déjà Views. Papers and dog-theme die cuts are all by Canson. **19** This is a page made for Karen and her family to remember just some of her many, many pets! Clip art saying from D.J. Inkers by Dianne J. Hook. Paper strips cut with Fiskars Wave Paper Edgers. **20** Jumpin' Grasshoppers pop-up page created with a Pebbles Tracer for letters and funky designs. Photos are cropped, with a Déjà Views Oval template, or matted using a Fiskar Paper Edger. This is one cool page! Four stars!

TIP: Use Fiskars Corner Edgers to customize mats.

TIP: Use our Resource Guide in the back of the book to find out how to own the creative products we have used throughout this publication!

© Hallmark

TIP: Use a small sponge colored with markers to add color to die cuts or backgrounds.

TIP: Use rubber stamps to embellish your die cuts and scrapbook pages. Experiment with different colors of embossing powders and inks on a variety of paper colors and textures.

TIP: Webster's definition of Scrapbook (skrap-book) n. a book of blank pages for mounting newspaper clippings, pictures and souvenirs, etc.; it Webster only knew what the scrapbook has become!

TIP: Collect and share punches, rubber stamps and scrapbooking tools with other scrapbooking friends.

TIP: Make a big statement in a little way. Contact Scrapbook Specialties to get a variety of mini-template sizes to make little scrapbooks. They even have the 2" templates to make albums that you can wear around your neck on a chain. Great gifts!

TIP: Cut-It-Up has a book called "Pop-It-Up" which features dozens of pop-up pages!

37

cute
as
a
bug

Mason and Nicole growing up together ~ more than friends... they are brother and sister, buddies, sweethearts. To them the world is at it's best!!!

32
USA

Children

MEMORIES

In my heart there lies an album
Which grows dearer every day
With the very special memories
That I've safely tucked away.

Though time looks to the future
And swallows up the past
It cannot fade nor take these
For I've put them there to last.

I just turn back the pages
And there I still can see—
The innocence within your eyes
As you looked up at me...

All the smiles, cheers and laughter—
Of childhood days too soon are gone
But those memories forever—
In my heart will linger on.

It's love that has the power—
To hold these things in place
All the beautiful reflections—
That time cannot erase.

My heart's album still lies open
With many pages yet to fill
For as long as love surrounds me—
Precious memories always will...

Excerpts from "Memories," a poem by Linda A. Jones, Treasured Reflections.
Copyright 1998. All rights reserved.

Photo opposite: "Cute As A Bug" made with Spot Lettering templates by Déjà Views.
Circle cut with a Fiskars Circle Cutter. Border created with a Déjà Views template edge.

39

The Watermelon was sweet...

Summer Fun

but not as sweet as our

FRIENDSHIP

You color our WORLD

Favorite shots at Two

FUN AT THE

ASPEN, CO. '98

KACEY

FOUNTAIN!

You're in the Spotlight!

Duck, Duck, Goose!

A little bread for you.

All lined up like baby ducks

Mr. Goose

aW SHUCKS

the only thing more fun than shucking it is...

WATER FUN

1	2	3
4	5	6
7	8	9

TIP: Slice sections of a photo into graduated strips to show action or movement; make sure to use a trimmer to be accurate!

1 Make juicy watermelon frames by cutting large green circles, smaller circles in white, then the smallest size in red or pink. Each circle should only be one half inch smaller. Your photo is the smallest size of all. Cut them all in half with a trimmer and layer on top of each other. Add details.

2 Hand-cut palette, brush and splotches of paint. Use stencils to make your title. Or just use a brush tip marker to make it look as if it was done by a little artist.

3 Film strips made with a Punchline punch which is available through Family Treasures. Photos are cropped with a Marvy Uchida Corner Rounder. Learn a variety of ways to mat photos using different tools, to make your scrapbook unique.

4 Paper Patch patterned paper used for background splashes and letters. Water droplets were created using Tsukineko opaque daubers and a stencil. Lettering created with a Pebbles Tracer.

5 Hollywood spotlight was hand-cut with scissors and a craft knife. Stars were made with Marvy Uchida punches. Photo in center was cropped with a Fiskars Circle Cutter. All paper by Canson.

6 Camera, filmstrips, hearts and stars are Accu-Cut die cuts and were used to frame the snapshot. Stars and Border gold embossed rubber stamp is by Denami Design and was used as a border to enhance the photo.

7 Patterned paper by Paper Patch. Déjà Views template was used to crop photo. The fancy Mini Pinking edge was created with Fiskars Paper Edgers by slowly cutting around the perfect oval shape. Lettering done with a white Zig Opaque Writer.

8 This sweet page was created using a Pebbles Funky Tracer for lettering. Yellow check paper is by Paper Patch and cut with Fiskars Blossom Paper Edgers to create an ear of corn. Solid colored paper by Canson. Lettering on bottom done with a Zig Opaque Writer

9 The garden hose is cut from Canson paper and complemented with big water drops. Letters created with paper by Paper Patch. Fiskars Paper Edgers used to cut mats. Fiskars Circle Cutter made all the perfect circles.

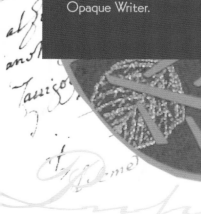

10 11
12 13

10 Paper and Sticky Die Cuts—both by Provo Craft. Stick your die cuts onto paper and trim around them before you adhere them to patterned paper. Lettering was done with Déjà Views Sticky Designer Letters. **11** A Mix n' Mat template made this page (including its border). Accu-Cut die cut letters created the word "Buddies." **12** Page layout was created using paper by Canson and Accu-Cut die cut shapes. This is a great page to feature a scavenger hunt or pirate birthday party. **13** Torn paper and Fiskars Ripple Paper Edgers were used to mat photos. Accu-Cut die cuts are sold by Cut-It-Up in a Pirate-themed package for all your little mates. Lettering created with Zig pens.

CHILDREN

Kori takes Aim

We all had such a blast at the

FUN FAIR

playing games,
winning prizes, eating ice
cream, and just being together!

Kristen hits the Bullseye!

We had YoYo contests seeing
who could sleep the YoYo the
very longest...We tied twice!
Micheal got me a new YoYo
when I went to visit him
in Atlanta!!

We timed it 58 seconds
was the tie breaker!
Wow, it will be hard to
t that!

Kori & Hannah

Johnny and

Hangin' out in the

TREEHOUSE

This little piggy....

stole my heart!

14 Make a bright-colored dart board from various sized circles using a Fiskars Circle Cutter. Stars and hearts made from Marvy Uchida punches. "Fun Fair" lettering created with Zig Opaque Writers. Mats for photos cut with Fiskars Scallop Paper Edgers.   **15** These unique little photo corners were made using Mix n' Mat templates. Letters by Accu-Cut in Scrapbook font. Finishing touches completed with Fiskars Heartbeat Paper Edgers. Use a pencil to trace a wavy ruler and document your photos with acid-free pens using the lines you just made. Don't forget to erase the pencil lines when you complete your journaling.   **16** Letters cut from Canson Paper using a Pebbles Log Cabin Tracer. Plaid paper by Paper Patch. Woodgrain paper by Provo Craft. Clouds created by silhouette-cropping the top of the photo into cloud shapes.   **17** Paper by Paper Patch. Heart die cut by Accu-Cut. Sweet snapshot!

| 14 | 15 |
| 16 | 17 |

TIP: Notice how the sidewalk was cropped and then continued on in paper to build a background for snapshots!

TIP: Take a look at "The Doctor Is In." Consider hanging any of your titles like a sign on the page; complete with string and nail!

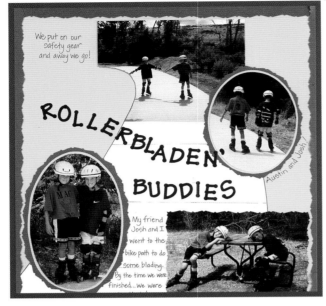

We put on our safety gear and away we go!

ROLLERBLADEN' BUDDIES

Austin and Josh!

My friend Josh and I went to the bike path to do some blading. By the time we were finished...We were

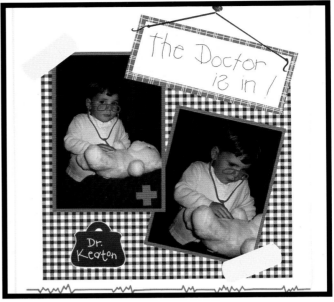

The Doctor is in !

Dr. Keaton

Hand in Hand

Johnny and GeGe stop to pose for a picture while on the way to find cool rocks and things along the Gunnison River

Side by Side ~

Kori + Jordan

I ♥ art.

"see my masterpiece?"

18 **19**
20 **21**

18 Paper by Canson, Designer Letters by Déjà Views, and Bowtie Paper Edgers by Fiskars were all that was needed for this page concept. **19** Patterned paper by Paper Patch and MPR and Associates' Paperbilities III. Doctor bag and bandages were hand-cut. **20** These beautiful black and white photos deserve special treatment! Border was traced with a Déjà Views ruler. Watercoloring creates a soft effect to match the tranquil mat which was created with a Déjà Views template edge. Photos trimmed with a Marvy Uchida Corner Rounder. **21** All paper by Canson. Embossing done with a Pebbles Funky Tracer. Stickopotamus stickers and a Déjà Views ruler worked well together to create the right-hand border. Heart-punched shapes by Marvy Uchida.

TIP: Déjà Views Viewlers and Rule-It-Up Rulers will make you an artist. Buy 'em and try 'em!

TIP: Ants, watermelon and picnic tablecloths are a creative backdrop for picnic photographs.

TIP: Add a lock of your child's hair—tied with a little snippet of pretty ribbon—to make a sweet child's layout.

22 Paper Patch paper. Fiskars Paper Edgers and Mrs. Grossman's stickers were used in this page design. Ant die cuts by Ellison. **23** This cute page uses paper by Canson and Paper Patch. Lettering was created with a white colored pencil from Zig's Memory Series. Torn mats, made with an Art Deckle ruler and layered on black paper with black photo corners by Canson, create a timeless look. **24** Background paper by Canson. Hand print rubber stamp by Inkadinkado. Acid-free doily by Elhers Company, Inc. Imports. Patterned paper by Paper Patch. Border created using a Déjà Views ruler traced with a Zig pen. **25** Page created using a Puzzlemate Template by Quick Cuts. Border cut with Mammoth Accents Scissors by Paper Adventures. Alison Nunley, Puzzlemates designer, made this page.

22	23
24	25

TIP: When dry paper embossing, use Canson's textured paper for a dimensional effect. Don't forget to first rub the area of paper you're going to emboss with waxed paper. This allows your stylus to glide easily as it presses into the design.

45

TIP: For elegant embossed mats: first, use a deckle-edged scissors to cut mat, then outline the edge with a thick-tipped embossing pen. Next, sprinkle with your favorite color of embossing powder and use a heat tool to make it rise. Beautiful!

26 Scrap pieces of paper were used in a pattern, then combined with Accu-Cut letters and punched shapes by Marvy Uchida. An ideal way to show off those special portraits. **27** Paper and white photo corners by Canson. Fiskars Deckle Paper Edgers trimmed the photo. The snowflakes were created by blending Canson die cut shapes, JudiKins and Personal Stamp Exchange snowflake rubber stamps, and the Family Treasures' large snowflake punch. **28** Paper by Canson. Frame decorated with stickers by Stickopotamus. Letters and football by Accu-Cut. **29** Peekaboo pages use two pages to document and feature full portraits. They make a great introduction page! Open up the sport page to reveal full portraits of Chase. Stickopotamus stickers, Accu-Cut stars and a helmet finish off this inspirational page.

TIP: When you start using the Puzzlemate Templates, it may be a little tricky to find perfect photos for every shape. Don't worry if you can't use every one for a photo. Use the remaining shapes to cut out solid or patterned paper. You may even use one to document your memories.

TIP: A star shape brightens up the O in Johnny.

30 Patterned paper by Paper Patch. Canson paper in black and white makes for a striking portrait page for Hannah. Lettering by Zig. **31** Accu-Cut letter stencil shapes backed with colored paper. Uchida punched and penned star shapes make the right-hand border. **32** Paper Patch plaid paper. Canson blue and white paper. Fiskars Deckle Paper Edgers used to trim mats. Canson photo corners make a classic-looking portrait page. Star Trio stamp by Rubber Stampede. Blue stars are hand-cut. Zig pens document the page and "stitch" a border. **33** Marvy Uchida's heart Corner Punch used to crop the mat. Blue mat was trimmed with Fiskars Nostalgia Corner Edgers. Inner white mat cut with Family Treasures' Jumbo Series, Antique Elegance Scissors; then, punched with McGill Punchline micro round and teardrop punches. All paper by Canson. Stamps matted onto paper cut with a Fiskars Stamp Paper Edger.

| 30 | 31 |
| 32 | 33 |

TIP: Ribbon can be added to a frame or mat for a finishing touch. Slit the paper with an exacto knife at 1" increments. Then, thread the ribbon through the slits and tie it to make a small bow. Sweet.

Baby Mitchell
FEB. 1992

give me Mr. Fuzzy   give me baba

now, give me remote control

Baby Boy

Baby

GOODNIGHT LITTLE ANGEL

The laughter has stopped dancing in his sleepy little eyes
And in the darkness I can hear his tiny little sighs
So innocent, he hugs my neck and dreams so peacefully
A little angel God has sent to share my world with me.

His head rests on my shoulder and I look into his face
And time has just stood still amid this humble little place
I realize with the humming of his quiet, breathless snore
He's filled my world with something I have never known before.

And then I have to wonder, as this angel clings to me
How did I get so lucky that I could get to be—
The one he reaches out to and needs so desperately
To guide his life and share his dreams and love so endlessly.
I softly whisper thank you as I kiss him on the head
I lay my angel down and then I tiptoe off to bed.

Excerpts from "Goodnight Little Angel," a poem by Linda A. Jones, Treasured Reflections.
Copyright 1997. All rights reserved.

Opposite page: K & Co. embossed scrapbook page.

TIP: Add "button holes" on punched shapes, and then embellish with pen for a border.

1 2 3
4 5 6
7 8 9

1 Border and rocking horse die cuts by Canson. The contrast of Canson's blue and yellow paper does a great job of setting off black and white photographs.

2 Bear frame punch and gold Metallic Gel Roller by Marvy Uchida. Baby-themed die cut shapes and background paper by Canson.

3 Alex Elshaw was featured using Accu-Cut letters and Canson papers. Mammoth Accent Scissors were used for the border. If you have favorite snapshots that don't fall under one theme, silhouette-crop them and place them in a patchwork of color!

4 Marilyn Eye cuddles her grandson! Special photos like this deserve a touch of paper embossing! One Heart, One Mind's—Fresh-n-Funky, multi-use stencil—used with a stylus and light box for embossing the frames. Paper by Paper Patch. Punched shapes by Marvy Uchida.

5 Designer Sticker Letters by Déjà Views. Lamb die cut and papers by Canson. Embossed border by Heritage Handcrafts. (Mount adhesive-backed die cut to colored paper and tear around the die cut. Then, layer onto several torn paper mats created with an Art Deckle ruler.)

6 Roses created by using the Quilts and Flowers Rule-It-Up Ruler by Cut-It-Up. For more Rule-It-Up ruler ideas look for "Rule It Up" by Tamara Sortman or "Rule It Up, Again" by Cut-It-Up. Border made with wide-tip calligraphy pen by Zig.

7 Decorative paper by Frances Myer. Déjà Views template used to cut ovals. Fiskars Deckle Scissors used to trim oval shape. Creative lettering done with Marvy Uchida's white Gel Roller.

8 Leaf and vine die cuts by Canson. Flowers were hand-cut. Then, a small punched center was added. Fiskars Arabian Paper Edgers were used. All patterned paper by Paper Patch.

9 Border made with Fiskars Ripple Paper Edger. Patterned Paper by Geopaper. Lettering done with a Zig Writer.

TIP: Try some of Canson's beautiful paper colors such as : Ivy, Amber, Canary, Buff, Hemp, Poppy, Violet, Red Earth and Twilight! Look for them in your local craft or fine art stores.

10 11
12 13

10 This sweet baby page was created by Sharon Kropp with Cut-It-Up's Lullaby Ruler ("Rule-It-Up"). You can use markers by Marvy Uchida on a round sponge to make the clouds. Embossed stars by Lasting Impressions brass template. Die cuts by Accu-Cut. Photos were trimmed with Marvy Uchida's Corner Rounder.
11 Lori featured her daughter CeCe on this adorable layout using baby-themed die cut shapes by Canson. Use soft-colored papers for the baby's first year - then break out the primarys! 12 Striped and patterned paper by Paper Patch. Star die cuts by Accu-Cut. Lettering by Pebbles Tracer. 13 Radio Flyer uses classic frames and photo corners to show off these cute black and white photographs! Lettering is hand done with Zig Memory Series pencils.

TIP: Create elegant simplicity by tearing paper. Torn paper adds a beautiful and unique dimension, achieved by no other technique.

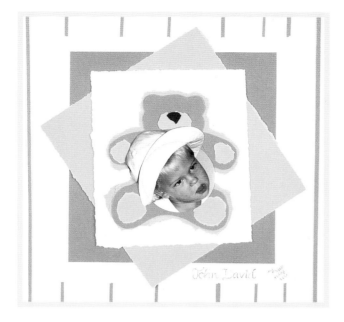

14 First, lay down strips of paper cut with a Fiskars trimmer. Then, tear a mat of champagne paper by Canson with an Art Deckle ruler. Use a self-adhesive die cut, or trace a bear shape from a template, and adhere it to paper. Ever so carefully, tear around your die cut shape leaving a soft edge. 15 Circular cropped photos and mats trimmed with a Fiskars Circle Cutter. A Pebbles Tracer template made the lettering. Lettering drawn with a Zig Opaque Writer. Die cut sun by Canson. 16 Splatter stamp image by Judy Pruitt of Straightforward Stamps. Lace Corner Punch by Family Treasures. Stickers by Provo Craft. Bottle shape was traced from template and torn for a softer effect! 17 Here are a few circle cutter ideas for you to try. Created with a Fiskars Circle Cutter, Mrs. Grossman's stickers, a Déjà Views ruler, white Zig Opaque Writer, Paper Patch and Canson Papers.

14 15
16 17

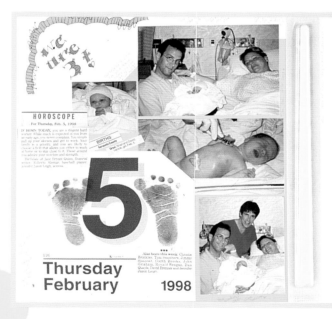

18	20
19	21 22

18 Decorative sticker letters by Melissa Neufield. Photos trimmed, cropped and matted with a trimmer by Fiskars. All paper by Canson. 19 A collage, photos, memorabilia and D.J. Inkers clip art made this double-page layout. 20 Shari used the Corner Rounder by Marvy Uchida to crop and trim photos, titles and memorabilia for baby Talia! 21 Silhouette cut your "little angels" and surround them with a hand-drawn frame & border. 22 Die cuts, border and papers by Hallmark.

OCT.- NOV. 1997

Dr. Mar-VU-Lous' Mad Scientist Kit #1: **Gravity!**

MAKING ROOM FOR BABY TALIA OR ALEX! DUE 2/4/98!

Every good and perfect gift is from above.

Christmas 1997

RUB - A - DUB - DUB!

...GOT MY Jansen in the TUB!

Quack Quack Quack Quack

TIP: A Marvy Uchida Corner Rounder is a must for speed scrapping!

TIP: Don't let old lettering standards cramp your creativity; get lettering books like Sandy Tyson's "Alphabet Soup Series" and have fun!

55

Children are a Gift of God .

| 23 | 25 |
| 24 | 26 |

23 & 24 Collage is a great technique to use when every photo is just too cute to exclude from your book of memories. Feature a little clip art here and there from D.J. Inkers by Dianne J. Hook. 25 Flower shapes were cut using a Rule-It-Up Ruler from Cut-It-Up. 26 "Kate" is written in Lindsay Ostrom's Picot Ribbon technique. Learn how to make this and dozens of other creative lettering styles step-by-step in "L,M,N,O,P More Creative Lettering with Lindsay."

TIP: They say "A picture is worth a thousand words." But photos can be worthless without words—Include handwritten notes, or your valuable memories could be lost forever.

TIP: Clip art makes you an artist; there is a theme for every page.

Garden Kids

The joyous combination of youth and fresh air put a skip in their step and a whistle in the wind. They were spirited and carefree. The sun was warm on their backs and a gentle breeze carried the scent of apple blossoms. A small ,cleared patch of soil in the corner of the yard was bursting with promise. That day you began to teach them that a loving hand and a nurturing heart are essential ingredients for healthy growth. They began to learn that with patience and perseverance, great is the reward in life and in a garden.

The masterful combination of nature and nurturing grew those flowers as they stretched for the sky to color God's great canvas. A sweet little garden provided a private corner of the world for teddy bear picnics. It's a place to share secrets and ponder life's infinite questions and perhaps someday pick a bridal bouquet. It is there you go to remember.

You planted seeds that day; in the ground... and in their hearts.

Opposite: Newport Albums by Kolo. Paper by Canson. Butterfly, Watering Can, Honey Bee and "We don't remember the days" rubber stamp by Personal Stamp Exchange. Lettering done with a gold Zig Opaque Writer. Foil corners by Ehlers Company Inc., Imports.

MEMORIES ARE LIKE FLOW-
ERS, THAT GOD PLANTS IN
OUR HEARTS — THAT BLOOM
AND FILL OUR LIVES WITH
LOVE AS THE YEARS GO BY.

BERRY PICKING

The girls are...

"See ya .."

Heading home...

OXOXOX OX OXO

Madeline Kay 7mos. Aug. 1998

I saved some Seeds...

My Little
Sunflower Patch

Summer '98

Jessica carefully helping with the herbs

August 1998

Sarah & Jessica playfully enjoying each other in the barnyard!

LIFE IS A FLOWER...

... OF WHICH LOVE IS THE HONEY!

cherries are for eating

Climbed the ladder for these great big cherries at Nani's honey!!

Mr. McGreggor's Garden

1 2 3
4 5 6
7 8 9

Rosemary

TIP: Zig White Opaque Writer is perfect for dark colored papers or black pages.

1 Paper and photo corners by Canson. Mat cropped with a Fiskars Paper Edger. Gold embossed aspen leaf stamp by Northwoods. Strawberries created by combining a sun and heart punch by Marvy Uchida. Berries made from patterned paper by Paper Patch. Green paper by Canson.

2 Barn was hand cut. Stenciling done with a Provo Craft Laser Stencil. All paper by The Paper Company. White lettering and embellishments created with a gel roller by Marvy Uchida.

3 Cropping and matting flower shapes was completed with a template by Provo Craft. Denim paper by Frances Meyers, Inc. Patterned paper by Over the Moon Press.

4 This page was created with solid green paper by Canson and patterned paper by Paper Patch. Sunflower seeds were saved in a Déjà Views 3-D Keeper. Photos cropped with a template by Déjà Views and a Circle Cutter by Fiskars. Letters cut using a template by Pebbles Tracer.

5 Pebbles templates and Cherished Memories stencils helped to create the soft borders. A Déjà Views template cut out the sun shape.

6 Paper by The Paper Company. A Pebbles stencil was used to make the bottom border.

7 Yellow paper by Canson. Patterned "Scrap Happy" paper by Design Originals. Flowers are hand cut. Embossed bee and flower created with template by Pebbles. Photos cropped and matted with template by Déjà Views. Corner Rounder by Marvy Uchida.

8 "Cherries Are for Eating" cut from Paper Patch paper using a Pebbles Template. Photos and mats cropped with a Fiskars Circle Cutter. All solid paper by Canson. Sweet page!

9 Fence was made using a Déjà Views ruler. Paper by The Paper Company. The adorable garden was created with die cuts by Canson. Oval cropped with a template by Déjà Views and trimmed with a Fiskars Paper Edger.

TIP: Try creating an album where one page is black and one white; alternate this throughout the entire album.

TIP: You will be delighted when you reproduce these pages and realize the richness of pages crafted with quality paper alone!

10 | 11
12 | 13

10 Sunflower is hand-cut. Letters by Accu-Cut. Mrs. Grossman's ladybugs are walking across the leaves. All paper by Canson. All pen embellishment and lettering done using Zig pens. **11** Paper and die cuts by Canson. Flowers painted with watercolors. Mats trimmed with Victorian Paper Edgers by Fiskars. **12** Artistic pen embellishment courtesy of Lindsay Ostrom. Sunflower stickers are by Mrs. Grossman's. Pitcher is an Accu-Cut die cut. **13** Paper by Paper Patch. Flowers created using Family Treasures' punches. Photo corners by Canson. Zig pens were used to create lettering.

Time to Harvest!

Bean

FREDONIA SEEDS

Sarah & Jessica snapped beans for hours!

- Summer - 1998 -

Carrot
Chantenay Red Cored

Michael digs in deep. Soon it will be time to water our gardens.

How does my garden grow?

The breaking of ground.

In every field of flowers, there's a little bit of Sunshine!

"Malin"~ Melon

Madeline Kay Malone 6 months old visiting Montrose July 1998

14 Die cut shapes by Canson. Marvy Uchida's white gel roller outlined all the photos. Paper by The Paper Company.   **15** Carrot top was hand cut from paper by Canson. Lettering created with Zig pens. Add seed packets for character on a garden page.   **16** Canson paper, Marvy Uchida's Corner Rounder and a Fiskars Blossom Paper Edger combined to make this gorgeous little garden page.   **17** Photos and mats cropped with a Fiskars Circle Cutter and then layered to make a watermelon patch. Pink check paper by Frances Meyer, Inc. White border created with a Fiskars Pinking Paper Edger.

14	15
16	17

Note: don't let acidic memorabilia touch any photos!

TIP:

18 "Sarah in the garden" photos were trimmed using a Marvy Uchida Corner Rounder. All die cut shapes by Canson. **19** Hallmark scrapbooking products were used for this layout. Hallmark makes border stickers—adhesive-backed for easy application. **20** All die cut shapes by Canson. Light rubber-stamped designs were used for the mat. The brown leaf die cut was stamped and embossed in gold. This beautiful page features Lindsay collecting her leaves and journaling. **21** Die cuts by Accu-Cut. Flowers are from the Mrs. Grossman's collection. Lettering created by Lindsay Ostrom with Zig pens.

Ladybug, ladybug, fly away home...

22 "Little Ladybug Abigail" was matted onto Frances Meyer's black and white checked paper. Blue and white Paperbilities III paper by MPR and Associates. Duplication of the trim on her dress creates a "one of a kind" border at the bottom. Ric-rac made with Fiskars Dragonback Paper Edger. Lady bugs by Mrs. Grossman's. **23** Paper by Geographics. Photos were silhouette-cropped. **24** A special page for Leah created by Mom. Patterned paper by Paper Patch. Petals were hand cut. "Leah" was written with a Zig Opaque Writer. **25** This sweetheart of a garden page was completed using a Puzzlemate Template by Quick Cuts, white background mat created by a Fiskars Imperial Paper Edger.

22	23
24	25

26 Border design created with a Fiskars Rotary Cutter with a Squiggle Blade. Flowers were designed using punches from Family Treasures. Lettering created with a white Zig Opaque Writer on violet paper by Canson. **27** Lace border created using the Ehlers Company, Inc. Imports acid-free lace doily. Page designed using the Puzzlemate Template by Quick Cuts. Paper Edgers by Fiskars. **28** The birdhouses were all hand cut from paper by Paper Patch or The Paper Company. Fence drawn using a Déjà Views Ruler and detailed with a Zig pen. Sunflower, vine and bird stickers by Mrs. Grossman's. **29** "Cute As A Bug" created with a Spot Lettering Template by Déjà Views. Border made using a Déjà Views template edge from the Mix n' Mat template. All design work accomplished with Zig pens.

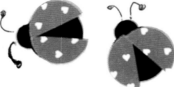

TIP: Jour·nal (jur´ nel) n. a daily record of events and happenings.

30 This very cute garden pop-up page was created using die cuts by Accu-Cut. Photos cropped with a template from Déjà Views. Photos trimmed with Marvy Uchida's Corner Rounder. Lettering created with a Zig Opaque Writer. **31** &32 Canson pages, photo corners and die cuts. Lettering created using Marvy Uchida's white gel roller. Sarah and Jessie are the perfect little models in the garden, since every move they make seems to be a picture worth keeping!

cousins

friends!

of friends

kind of

are the best

Cousins

You share a unique bond forged in family. Always, you feel that connection despite your distinct differences. They're your cousins and at times even closer than a brother or sister.

Your cousin mirrors your gestures and yet you're both still surprised every time it happens! Genuine laughter reminds you that the best friends can be found in your own family. You've played make-believe and dress-up, connected with nature on a down-to-earth camping trip and whispered secrets since you were small. Slumber parties taught you that popcorn and heart-to-heart talks lasting late into the night are truly important.

A plan for the next adventure is always taking shape. You really should take that trip together and visit the sweet little antique shop you went to last summer. Also, there are times when simply being together on a lazy afternoon is enough. Cherish each memory together.

Cousins Sarah and Lindsay

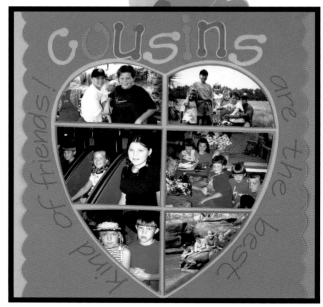

Cousins are the best kind of friends!

COUSINS ARE THE BEST!

Aunt Jodi took us all out boating and tubing on Lake La Femme Dieu I love going to Minnesota and spending time with my cousins!

JD yells "HIT IT"/

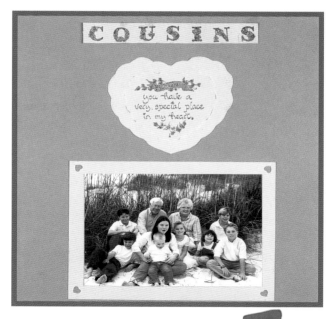

COUSINS

you have a very special place in my heart.

1 2 5
3 4

a b c d e f g h i j k
l m n o p q r s t u v
w x y z

1 Border and embellishments designed using Zig pens and a Déjà Views ruler and Doodad. Mint green paper by The Paper Company. Bright green paper by Canson was used as a mat for the page. Photos were trimmed with a Corner Rounder by Marvy Uchida. **2** The word "cousins" was cut from Canson's bright-colored paper using a Déjà Views Spot Lettering Template. Paper Adventures Mammoth Accent Scissors made the nice long cuts of paper for the borders, almost like "a ruler in a scissor." Puzzlemate's heart-shaped template created this layout of the cousins having fun over the summer. Paper by Canson. Lettering by Zig pens. **3** The wave die cuts layered in shades of blue create the lower border. The waves and anchor die cuts by Accu-Cut. Paper by Canson. Top border was made using a Fiskars Rotary Cutter and a Wave blade. **4** The word "cousins" is made with Hero Arts Rubber Stamps, then embossed and colored in with Zig markers. The die cut has been embossed with a template as well as a rubber stamp. The photo was matted on a piece of paper trimmed with a heart punch. **5** Puzzlemate template by Quick Cuts. Paper Adventures Mammoth Accents Scissors were used on the border. A star punch by Marvy Uchida was punched directly into the photos to enhance layout.

TIP: If you haven't had the pleasure of using a Fiskars rotary cutter; try to beg, borrow, or buy one and experiment! They are a quick and easy tool for making borders and mats. A variety of decorative blades make them incredibly versatile. There is even a perforation blade to add dimension to your die cuts and paper shapes. (Our favorites are the Tiara and Squiggle blades.)

TIP: Create a scrapbook easily by just keeping a journal, then occasionally add a few snapshots and memorabilia. Great for a vacation keepsake!

There is a time for everything, and
a season for every activity under
heaven.

Ecclesiastes 3:1

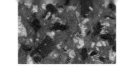

Seasons

We saw the coolest rainbow on our way to the lake. We stopped to play in the rain and take pictures! How pretty is that?

TO EVERYTHING THERE IS A SEASON.

Leaf piles are for jumping, water is for splashing and snow was sent especially for making snowmen. The expectation of each season embraces a new beginning for people of all ages. Seasons segment the years reminding us to preserve precious memories while time marches on. Spring reminds us to nurture our families and help them grow. Every summer we remember the smells of fresh-cut grass and barbecues, the sight of the night exploding with fireworks and the chill of the last swim of the season. Fall brings brilliant foliage and walks through the woods to find leaves for pressing. Winter is a contrast of crunchy cold mornings and warm wool blankets, snowball fights and crackling fires. The changing seasons whisper "time is passing; you'll want to remember this moment."

Opposite page: This page designed using Canson paper and die cuts highlighted with an Opaque Writer pen by Zig.

73

Rare Rainy Days in Colorado

Laura (8), Micah (5), "Honey Alli" (2) & Maya Curtis (5) — Summer of 1989 - Montrose

Barefoot in the Rain

Cobin and Carter

come rain or

come shine! 3-Year-Old Micah

outside in my neighborhood

our little

snow star

My little red sled and away I go!

Happy Golden Days

OCT '82

Kacey

Enjoying the Fall Colors

We stopped on Kebler Pass to look at the pretty colors and tromp through the leaves. I love this time of year!

TRIPLE THE FUN

Tia

Tiffany

Tyrell

Cousins in Summer

Lindsey and Sarah in Grandma's Garden up at the lake in Minnesota ~ 1975 ~

TIP: Try rolling your borders with Clearshop's Rollergraph System.

1	2	3
4	5	6
7	8	9

TIP: For fun, take some pictures on a rainy day.

1 Hand-cut umbrella and raindrops from Canson paper. Border lines created with Zig Opaque Writer.

2 Lettering created with a Tracer by Pebbles. Paper by Canson. Barefoot embossing template by Lasting Impressions. Corrugated-looking paper by Paper Pizazz from H.O.T.P.

3 Canson paper and sun die cuts were mixed with imagination! Rainy day photos are so sweet and special and little people have a delightful time posing.

4 "Our little Snowstar" page was created with Paper Pizazz snowflake paper from H.O.T.P. Déjà Views templates were used to crop star shapes. Pebbles Tracer created letters.

5 Hand lettered with Zig Opaque Writer. Solid-colored paper and photo corners by Canson. Patterned paper by Over the Moon Press. Wheat shaft was stored in a Déjà Views 3-D Keeper.

6 Sweet Kacey is nestled in the leaves made with punches by Family Treasures. Denim paper by Frances Meyer, Inc. Tan, wrinkled-look paper by Geographics.

7 Paper, photo corners and leaf die cuts by Canson. Déjà Views Designer Sticker Letters used for the title. A Fiskars Crimper was used to give leaves texture.

8 Lettering created with Zig Opaque Writer. Photos and papers were trimmed with Marvy Uchida's Corner Rounder. Oak leaf die cuts and paper by Canson.

9 Clearsnap Rollergraph System "rolled out" the stamped border (embossed gold). Both herb stamps by Stampington & Company.

TIP: Canson paper shapes are all adhesive-backed. They are wonderful to work with because you just peel and stick.

TIP: The more you experiment and learn about tools, the more fun you'll have making your treasured albums!

TIP: Marvy Uchida's Corner Rounder is the best speed tool for trimming and matting.

9 Each Puzzlemate Template by Quick Cuts has its own unique patterns for layouts. Your challenge is finding photos that will work within the template shapes! Play around and experiment with different photos to see what works best . The time is well spent ...every page turns out perfectly! **10** This "Fall Family Fun" page was lovingly created by Cindi Byers. She used templates by Déjà Views and die cuts by Canson for the leaves. Photo corners by Canson. **11** Template shapes by Déjà Views. Border cut with Paper Adventures Mammoth Accents Scissors. Leaf stickers by Stickopotamus. Top photo trimmed with a Fiskars Summit Corner Edger. Bottom photo trimmed with Paper Edgers by Fiskars. Paper by Canson. **12** "Pumpkin Patch" was created using Paper Patch patterned paper with Canson paper and die cut shapes. Designer sticker letters by Déjà Views.

TIP: Papers by Catherine has a unique and beautiful paper assortment. Perfect for your scrapbook!

13 Canson pumpkin and leaf shapes were mounted onto a square patchwork of color! The paper layers add dimension. All paper by Canson.   14 Solid colored paper by Canson. Writing created with Zig Opaque Writers. Photos cut with a Fiskars Circle Cutter. The word "Fall" is cut from an extra snapshot using a Pebbles Tracer. Leaf paper by Paper Pizazz from H.O.T.P.   15 All paper and shapes by Canson. Here is a fun technique you will use time and again; mount your die cuts onto colored paper and "stitch" around them! 16 Oak leaf and "Friends are forever" saying by Personal Stamp Exchange. Lettering created with Zig pens. This torn paper shows well; it is adhered to a darker color for contrast. Leaf paper from Papers by Catherine. Photo corners by Canson.

| 13 | 14 |
| 15 | 16 |

TIP: Mount your die cut letters onto another color then trim around them before applying to your page.

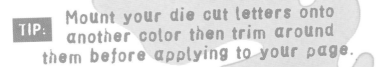

Autumn Gold

Be exalted,
O God, above
the heavens;
Let your glory
be over all
the earth.
Psalm 57:11

Keaton explores
in a beautiful
January snowfall

1997

winter

Pumpkin
Patch

Let's
Ski

Let it snow!

Herbal

NOTE: A special thanks to Canson for donating blank scrapbook pages and beautiful, colored papers.

| 18 | 19 |
| 20 | 21 |

TIP: Find out the latest, hottest scrapbooking news. Join the International Scrapbook Trade Association (972) 318-0492.

18 Maple leaf rubber stamp by Personal Stamp Exchange. Paper by Canson. 19 White snowflake paper by Paper Pizazz from H.O.T.P. Photo corners by Canson. "Winter" cut from a Pebbles in my Pocket Tracer. Large snowflakes were made with a Denami Design rubber stamp. Blue snowflake paper by Paper Patch. Fiskars Paper Edgers were used to trim the mat. Photo corners by Canson. Use the diamond shape from a Déjà Views template to create a snowflake from paper and a snapshot! 20 "Pumpkin Patch" lettering by Accu-Cut. Patterned paper by Paper Patch. Die cut shapes by Canson. 21 Paper shapes and photo corners by Canson. Large snowflake by Denami Design rubber stamp. Small snowflake by Provo Craft stickers. Photo trimmed with a Fiskars Ripple Paper Edger.

TIP: Try rubber stamping with the Adirondack Collection of earth-toned colors from Ranger.

TIP: If you've made a few extra-special pages you treasure, shrink them down to 3"x 3" and laminate them to make a key chain. Great gift!

TIP: Silhouette-cut your little snow bunnies and place them on a torn paper mountain!

TIP: Chronicle your heartaches and disappointments along with your celebrations and joys. They are all a precious part of who you are.

Holidays

Year to year, when it comes time for Christmas, everyone is excited— especially us kids. It's a time when families usually get together. My relatives often visit during the holidays. Christmas Eve is our big day. Usually a ham or turkey is served with all the fixin's. We kids never eat much. We are too excited about our presents. After tummies are "full" and plates cleaned, the dishes must be done. The kids quickly clear the table while the grown-ups do the dishes. Then, we all crowd around the Christmas tree. Two or three kids are assigned the duty of present passer-outers. Sometimes we try to sneak a peak, but are kindly reminded to wait until all of the gifts have been passed out. Then, when Grandpa gives the word, the real fun begins. The whole room is filled with the sound of paper tearing, as everyone opens their gifts. Everyone that is, except... Grandma. Grandma, who is voted every year as "most present giver" watches her six grandchildren as they open their gifts. When, and only when, the last child has opened the last present (and given Grandma a last thank-you hug), does she open hers— slowly but surely, being careful to save the wrapping paper. When Grandma opens her presents, everybody watches. And, everybody ohhs and ahhs. Christmas at my house is a wonderful, family get -together—full of love.

By Lindsay Haglund, Age 12.

Opposite page: K & Co. embossed scrapbook page.

1 Braid border created with a Fiskars Circle Cutter. Cut multiple circles from three colors, cut into quarters and fit together as shown. Letters and Christmas ornament cut by hand.

2 Letters by Making Memories. Notice that layering contrasting colors of letters creates a shadow effect. Easter egg stickers by Mrs. Grossman's. Basket by Azadi. Bunny is a fabric doily. Border made with a Déjà Views template.

3 Designed with a Puzzlemate template by Quick Cuts. Border cut with Paper Adventures Mammoth Accents Scissors. Paper by Canson.

4 All paper die cut shapes and words by Accu-Cut. The border was cut using a Déjà Views Ruler. Photo was cropped with a Déjà Views template.

5 All die cut shapes and words by Accu-Cut. Photo and mats trimmed with Paper Edgers by Fiskars and a Marvy Uchida Corner Rounder. Paper by Canson. Pen embellishments done with a Marvy Uchida gel roller.

6 Die cut shapes and words by Accu-Cut. Solid-colored paper by The Paper Company.

7 These pages affectionately display special friends' Christmas photos from the mailbox. When they arrive, put them straight into an album and feature it on your coffee table all season! Christmas die cuts by Canson.

8 All patterned paper by Paper Patch. Die cut shapes by Accu-Cut. Letters cut with a Pebbles Tracer. Red paper by Canson.

9 All die cut shapes and papers by Canson. Canson has partriotic die cuts that can be used for a variety of events.

TIP: Start with Canson adhesive-backed paper. Then, cut shapes with an Accu-Cut Roller Machine to make sticky die cuts.

TIP: Clip art allows everyone to be an artist. Trace artwork directly onto your scrapbook page with a lightbox and acid-free pens.

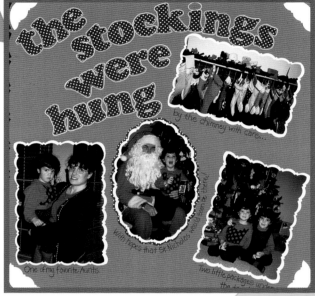

Fourth of July

Joy

TIP: Turn your black-and-white photos into colorful creations with Marshall's Photo Coloring System; Simple and elegant!

10 All die cut shapes and photo corners by Canson. Left border created with a Déjà Views Doodad. Lettering by C-Thru lettering templates. **11** Letters created with a Pebbles Tracer. Patterned paper by Paper Patch. Photographs and mats cut with a Fiskars Blossom Paper Edger. **12** All die cut shapes by Canson. Photos cropped with a Déjà Views Mix n' Mat and oval template. **13** Accu-Cut die cuts and paper. Photos trimmed with a Deckle Paper Edger by Fiskars.

84

TIP: Contrasting paper colors create a dramatic effect.

TIP: For large, decorative edges, use Paper Adventures Mammoth Accents Scissors; they make giant cuts. They're like "a ruler-in-a-scissors!"

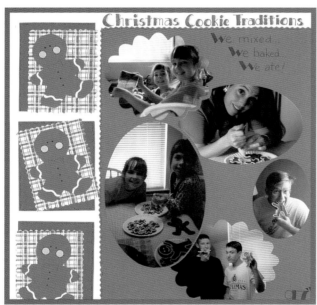

14 Border, Christmas tree and music note die cuts by Ellison. Stickers by Mrs. Grossman's. Trees were punched with small hand punches and layered to create star ornaments.   15 Accu-Cut die cuts. Stickers by Mrs. Grossman's. Creative lettering by Vicki Breslin.   16 Cute little gingerbread men cut using a cookie cutter! Photos trimmed with a Déjà Views template.   17 All gingerbread men by Ellison. Photos trimmed with a Marvy Uchida Corner Rounder. Lettering by Zig Opaque Writer.

| 14 | 15 |
| 16 | 17 |

 TIP: Look for and take candid photos to get unrehearsed reflections of life.

 TIP: Your photographs are priceless! Safely preserve and display them!

85

"We danced all night!"

"music is the voice of Love!"

"Cheek to Cheek"

Sweet Heart Dance

· OCTOBER 1998 ·

"Dining, Dancing, and Romancing"...

86

Music

Chunky little fists of a two-year-old banging on his first piano; a ten-year-old trumpet player practicing scales in his bedroom; and, the concert violinist performing at Carnegie Hall, all share something special...music. Music plays an integral role in our lives punctuating poignant moments; graduation day, weddings, the Fourth of July.

We mentally rewind and play the scenes of our lives simply by hearing a favorite song from times past.

Whether your family gathers washboards and spoons or your kids sing silly songs around the campfire, music brings people together. Composing the perfect piece or hitting the extraordinary high note is an admirable achievement, but for most of us, music means making a joyful noise that resonates in the heart.

Opposite: All products on this music scrapbook page are by Hallmark.

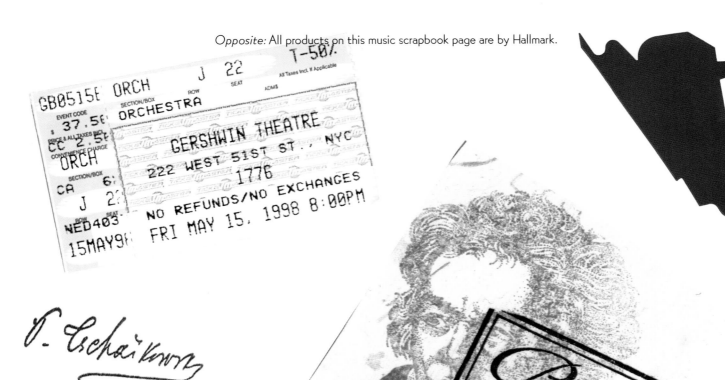

TIP: Did you know Provo Craft's Sticky Designer Die Cuts are repositionable for up to 30 minutes?

1 A Fiskars Ripple Paper Edger was used to make the photo mat. Border created with a Déjà Views Ruler. Paper by Geographics. Solid-colored paper by Canson. **2** Sheet music rubber stamp by Stampington & Co. Treble clef rubber stamp by Inkadinkado. Photos and mats trimmed with a Fiskars Summit Corner Edger. **3** Music-themed Sticky Designer Die Cuts by Provo Craft. Designer Letters by Déjà Views. Colonial and Arabian Paper Edgers by Fiskars were used to mat the photos and cut the border. **4** Lori Pieper created this spectacular page to encourage Johnny's musical talents by hand-cutting the piano keyboard. Die cut shapes by Accu-Cut. Photos trimmed with a Marvy Uchida Corner Rounder.

MARCH 1982

Sing...

5 A blank scrapbook page was left out after the concert and fans were encouraged to sign a page for memory's sake. Clip art from D. J. Inkers by Diane J. Hook. **6** All die cut shapes by Ellison. Paper by Canson. **7** Page created with Paper Piercing Patterns by Windows of Time. **8** Each special guest's snapshot was silhouetted to preserve his support of the Faithful 4 Quartet. Die cut shapes by Ellison.

5	6
7	8

Toccata in D Minor

Johann Sebastian Bach

Adagio molto

a Party for a Princess

You Are Invited

Recipe for Friendship
(Serves two)
3 cups kindness
2 cups understanding
1 heaping spoonful patience
Dash of playfulness
Season with smiles and laughter
Enjoy as often as possible!

Tea Time

It arrived on a delicate piece of torn paper, written in a gentle hue of blue crayon. It was simple and to the point, though it was just a few lines. I responded immediately to an invitation to tea.

Proper attire for this special event called for a vintage flair to help set the mood and enhance her efforts. I wore a floppy hat with a pale pink cabbage rose and an organdy ribbon with a long flowing dress. White gloves completed the ensemble.

She inherently displayed the hospitality of a more experienced hostess. Spontaneity hadn't hindered preparations. Her special touches sparkled on a table set with checkered cloth and two mismatched napkins. The tea set was silver and only absent a piece or two. A small china tray held cookies for us to share. Etiquette was important as we delicately placed our napkins on our laps.

We were kindred spirits sharing so much more than tea and cookies. We shared our hearts. She may have been only three, but to me she was as grand as her tea party.

Opposite Page: Designed with Accu-Cut die cuts and acid-free doilies from the Ehlers Company Inc., Imports.

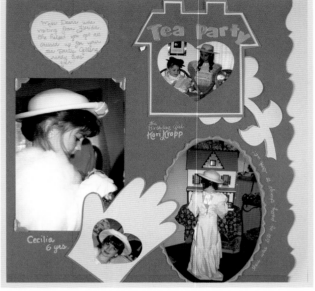

1 2 **3 4** Paper and die cut shapes by Canson. Words created with Zig pens and Déjà Views Designer Letters. Border designed with Ruler by Déjà Views. Photos have mats made by tearing Canson paper. **2** Sarah and Jessie's Tea Party memories were preserved on Keepsake paper from the "Scrap Happy" Collection by Design Originals. Acid-free doily is by Ehlers Company Inc., Imports. Photo corners by Canson. Mats were trimmed with a Fiskars Ripple Paper Edger. **3** Patterned paper by Paper Pizazz from H.O.T.P. Solid-colored paper by The Paper Company. Frames torn with an Art Deckle ruler from Canson paper. **4** Hand die cut is from Canson. All other die cuts sold by Cut-It Up. Wavy border created with a Déjà Views Ruler. Lettering done with a creative hand using Zig pens.

TIP: Plan a Tea Party with treats and dress-up clothes; then grab your camera.

5 The wooden spoon and mixing bowl were hand cut. The bowl trim was created using Déjà Views Mix n' Mat template edge. Photo trimmed with a Marvy Uchida Corner Rounder. Writing and bowl design created with Zig Opaque Writers.   6 The snapshot of Kacey, the little chef, has a torn paper mat and is mounted with Canson photo corners. Rolling pin, cooking mitt, and spoon were hand-cut from Canson and Paper Patch paper. Recipe matted using Fiskars Paper Edgers.   7 Hallmark makes die cut frames and tape borders for speed scrapbooking.   8 Bowl and spoon were hand-cut. "Lickin' the Spoon" photos cropped with a Déjà Views template. Paper by Paper Patch and Canson. Lettering done with Zig Opaque Writers.

Birthday

Whether you are young in years or simply young at heart, a birthday is a very special day. It's the celebration of life; the celebration of you. Birthdays recall the day you were born and warmly welcomed into the world.

Surrounded by family and friends, it's a day for pure amusement and memory-making events. Confetti and balloons dance in the air. Laughter, games with prizes, ice cream, cake and presents all sweeten your day. Freeze the memory; the glow of the candles as you blow them out, the funny gift from your high school girlfriend, the friend who came to surprise you. A birthday is the brightest day of the year swirled in a ribbon of happiness.

TIP: Using a mat and craft knife, carve designs out of your favorite patterned papers to create gorgeous frames for snapshots.

TIP: Zig has small writing booklets for each pen tip to help you create letters, borders and doodles.

1 Page created using a Rule-Up Ruler from Cut-It-Up. Designed by Vicki Breslin.

2 Dad's birthday page was created with Canson's paper, photo corners and die cuts. The border on the bottom was made with a Déjà Views Ruler.

3 Streamers made with a Fiskars Rotary Cutter. Mats trimmed with a Fiskars Blossom Paper Edger. Lettering made with a Pebbles Tracer. Writing by Zig Opaque Writer. Balloons formed with a Fiskars Circle Cutter.

4 The 50th birthday recollections were made using paper by Canson, Accu-Cut die cuts, and a Zig Opaque Writer. Bottom border birthday candles created using a Pebbles template.

5 Canson's self-adhesive die cuts create a whimsical birthday border for Dad's 70th birthday page. Border trimmed with a Fiskars Rotary Cutter. Oval cut with a Déjà Views template.

6 Mrs. Grossman's stickers and a Déjà Views template made Sarah's 5th birthday page. Circles cut with a Fiskars Circle Cutter.

7 Patterned paper by Paper Patch. Lettering by Accu-Cut. Die cut shapes by Canson and Accu-Cut. Solid-colored paper by Canson.

8 Paper Patch paper and Accu-Cut's "Happy Birthday" message jazz up these special snapshots. A template from Déjà Views was used to trim the oval photo.

9 Party popper and "Happy Birthday" by Accu-Cut. Frame and photo corners by Canson. Paper by the Paper Patch Company.

neutral
←acidic ↓ alkaline→ 14
0 ――― 7.0 ―――

TIP: Do you know why you're choosing acid-free products? 0=acidic 14=alkaline 7.0 is neutral or acid-free. The acid (as well as the wood pulp) in paper cause it to yellow, become brown and brittle. It also causes color to fade from photos.

10 Photos trimmed with a Fiskars trimmer. The stickers and border from Mrs. Grossman's made a great page for Jason. **11** This page was created to feature one special birthday photo. Snapshot was trimmed and double-matted with a Fiskars Trimmer, then mounted with Canson's photo corners. Die cuts by Canson. **12** Birthday pocket page was designed with Paper Patch Paper and Canson die cuts. Letters by Accu-Cut.

TIP: Think before you snap! Be a photojournalist and let the picture tell a story!

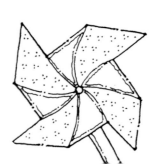

Make
A
Wish!

This was my best party ever! Grandma Haglund made a beautiful cake, and boy, was it ever yummy!!!

Ryan's Surprise 16th Birthday

GRANDSON, Hope your Birthday's great

HAPPY
BIRTHDAY

Sarah opening presents

Sarah and Rebeccah

13 Simple design made with a Fiskars trimmer. Paper and die cut by Canson. Lettering by Zig acid -free pens using a Chatterbox Journaling Genie template.   **14** Cindi Byers created this labor of love for her son Ryan. She used Canson die cuts and a Marvy Uchida Corner Rounder.   **15** Another Birthday pocket page created using balloon shapes cut from a template. Creative Letters by Making Memories. Patterned paper by Paper Patch.   **16** Birthday die cuts by Canson and Ruler by Déjà Views worked together to create this interesting border. Photos and mats cropped with a Marvy Uchida Corner Rounder and a Fiskars Circle Cutter.

14	15
16	

Beach

Do you remember your first trip to the beach? The vast expanse that stretched forever? Did the sun dance diamond—bright upon the water? Think back to the sand and the way it swallowed your toes as the waves lapped over them. The air was cool but the sand was warm. You constructed a veritable fortress of sand—so confident that it would stand forever. And, you felt the pangs of disappointment as the sea reclaimed your masterpiece.

Did you scour the shore for starfish and shells while the seagulls serenaded you in the open air? Did you taste the salt air and savor the flavors of hot dogs and root beer floats? Did you wish the day would never end? The pictures never will. They will endure, unlike footprints in the sand.....

Opposite page: Page created with Canson paper and die cuts.
Photos trimmed with a Fiskars Circle Cutter or a Marvy Uchida Corner Rounder

Lovely Lynda

a sunny day

on the beach

Abigail in Florida ~ Sept. 1998

Baseball on the beach

Florida 1998

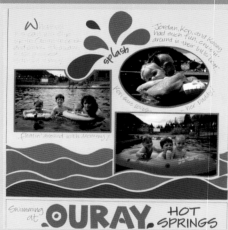

splash

Jordan, Ken, and Rosey had such fun cruisin' around in their little boat.

Swimming at OURAY HOT SPRINGS

Boating in Ft. Myers

On Sept. 5th ~spur of the moment~ we decided to drive straight through from Dallas to Ft. Myers, Florida to visit Great Grandma & Grandpa Taylor. Here were taking a boat ride on Alligator Bay.

COUSINS ARE THE BEST!

Aunt Jodi took us all out boating and tubing on Lake Latomme. Dieu I love going to Minnesota and spending time with my cousins!

SUMMER TIME

I found a starfish in the water see it in my hand.

Jason Lindsay at Grandma and Grandpa beach house in Florida.

My cousin Sara she loves swimming at the beach!

FLORIDA   Lindsay

Ribet.. Ribet.. Ribet.. Ribet. Ribet.. Ribet.. Ribet

Summer Swimmin with Jake!

I think I saw a SHARK!

All geared up and ready!

1 2 3
4 5 6
7 8 9

TIP: Remember, your children may love to scrapbook right along with you; keeping a memory album can be a family project!

TIP: Torn paper adds a whole new dimension to your scrapbooking; once you try it, you're hooked!

102

SUN

TIP: Look for "Scrapbooking for Kids (ages 1 to 100)", (another TweetyJill Publication) to learn about every tool and technique used for scrapbooking.

1 Lindsay Ostrom designed this scrapbook page. She used an Accu-Cut die cut sold by Cut-It-Up. Mrs. Grossman's stickers were used for the seascape.

2 A Sunny Day at the Beach was created with Accu-Cut letters. Paper and die cuts by Canson. The sunglass frame was made with a Fiskars Circle Cutter.

3 All paper shapes and paper by Canson. Lettering was done with a Zig Opaque Writer.

4 Waves were made with paper by Canson and a creative hand! A Déjà Views template was used to cut the oval. Letters created with a Pebbles Tracer.

5 Rope and flag created with a Pebbles template. The photos were single-matted with a Fiskars trimmer.

6 Large wave border and anchor die cut by Accu-Cut. Lettering drawn with Zig pens. Top border cut with Paper Adventures Mammoth Edge Accents Scissors.

7 This page was created by Matthew to remember his summertime day at the beach. Photo corners and die cut shapes are by Canson. Children love scrapbooking too, just give them a chance!

8 Mrs. Grossman's stickers add a touch of whimsy to this layout. The starfish is an Accu-Cut die cut.

9 Paper and die cut shapes by Canson. Marvy Uchida's Corner Rounder trimmed the photos. A Déjà Views ruler was used to create the wavy edge on the underwater snapshots.

TIP: Next time you have a vacation near the ocean, buy an underwater camera and take a few photos just for fun.

103

"I think I can..."

Keaton

Kori "surfing" in the river

Sand Dunes

Jake & lexi

at the beach

SAIL

WITH ME

Coastline Sunset

The remnants of our golden day together illuminate the sky...

10 **11**
12 **13**

10 Oval-shaped photos cut with a Déjà Views template. Paper and die cuts by Canson. Note how the photograph is sliced at intervals to create movement. Try this technique on a duplicate photo first!   **11** Die cut shapes by Accu-Cut. Stickers by Mrs. Grossman's.   **12** Flag, life preserver, anchor, ropes and the word "sail" were all created with Pebbles templates. All the details and lettering were made with an Opaque Zig marker.   **13** A simple hand-drawn coastline, sunset adds warmth to this sunset shot at the lake. Looks like an extra-special memory!

TIP: You can experience a flood of recollections from a simple keepsake; start a file just for collecting memorabilia!

14 Torn waves and a sand dune make these beach family portraits look beautiful! Die cuts and photo corners by Canson. Starfish, conch shell, and small sun symbol rubber stamps by Personal Stamp Exchange. Nautilus shell stamp by Rubber Stampede. **15** This simple page idea was created using a Fiskars trimmer for cropping and matting. Die cut shapes by Canson. Bottom right photograph trimmed using a Fiskars Corner Edger. **16** The letters in "Hawaii" and the embossed shapes were created with Pebbles templates. Paper and die cut shapes by Canson. **17** "Sun," "sand" and "smiles"—die cut letters by Accu-Cut. All die cut shapes by Canson. Border created with a Déjà Views template. Patterned paper by Paper Patch.

| 14 | 15 |
| 16 | 17 |

At The Beach

18	19
20	21

18 The waves in "H2O Fun" were created with Wave Paper Edgers by Fiskars. Paper and die cut shapes by Canson. Photos were trimmed using Marvy Uchida's Corner Rounder. Spiral and cross stamp by Judi-Kins. **19** Photos have been trimmed and cropped using a Corner Rounder by Marvy Uchida. Paper and die cuts by Canson. Bottom photo border collage created with a Déjà Views Ruler and multiple photos. A map and brochure were included to help tell the vacation story. **20** Two snapshots were highlighted with torn Caribbean Collection paper from Papers by Catherine. Palm tree rubber stamp by Stampington & Co. **21** Photos cropped with a Fiskars Circle Cutter. Mats trimmed with a Fiskars Ripple Paper Edger. Lettering was created using Zig Memory Series colored pencils.

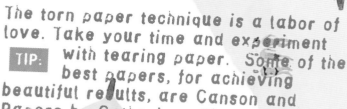

TIP: The torn paper technique is a labor of love. Take your time and experiment with tearing paper. Some of the best papers, for achieving beautiful results, are Canson and Papers by Catherine. These papers have longer fibers and leave a nice textured edge. You can do artistic pages with just torn paper, a rubber stamp and a few minutes of brainstorming.

22 Die cut frames and shapes from Canson make this a tropical paradise memory! Elements of a vacation brochure were used to enhance the page. Rubber stamp the images on Canson's self-adhesive die cuts before you peel them off. Friends are Forever stamp by Personal Stamp Exchange add interest to sun die cut. 23 "Sanibel Island" was lettered with Zig Memory Series colored pencils.

TIP: If you want to use souvenirs from your vacation, such as a brochure or map, be sure you don't let them come in direct contact with your photographs. Remember, they are made from acidic materials!

TICKETS PASSPORT

Born to Travel

Painting
grandma's
flower garden
June '96 Crasslake
Minnesota

Grandma
Knowlen
waters flowers.

Matthew in the
"tree horse" behind the
cabin at the lake.

CABIN

Lindsay and
Matthew love
grandma's
garden

Vacation

If you balloon in Burgundy, or trek in Nepal—if you camp at the lake, or head for the amusement park - it's a vacation. What a wild and wonderful word! Vacation means an escape from the routine—new places, friends and adventures. It conjures up images of food, fun, laughter and tacky souvenirs. It means time spent with you and your family creating important memories—beginning traditions that will endure for generations.

Vacations change the person within us. Aren't silly hats a travel prerequisite? We diligently write postcards to convince everyone that where we are is considerably better than where they are. And, we take pictures with people we don't even know! We cram a week's worth of activity into every day and come home... needing a vacation!

Opposite : page designed using paper and die cuts by Canson and a Fiskars Paper Edger. Simple watercolors make this a beautiful page.

109

You don't need to crop photos on every page.

TIP: The longer you scrapbook, the more you'll find ways to "Speedscrap"—combining super-easy pages with a few more time-consuming ones. It's the combination that's pleasing to the eye and keeps you committed to scrapbooking.

1	2	3
4	5	6
7	8	9

TIP: Add vacation brochures (or elements from them) to help tell your vacation story when you're missing photos.

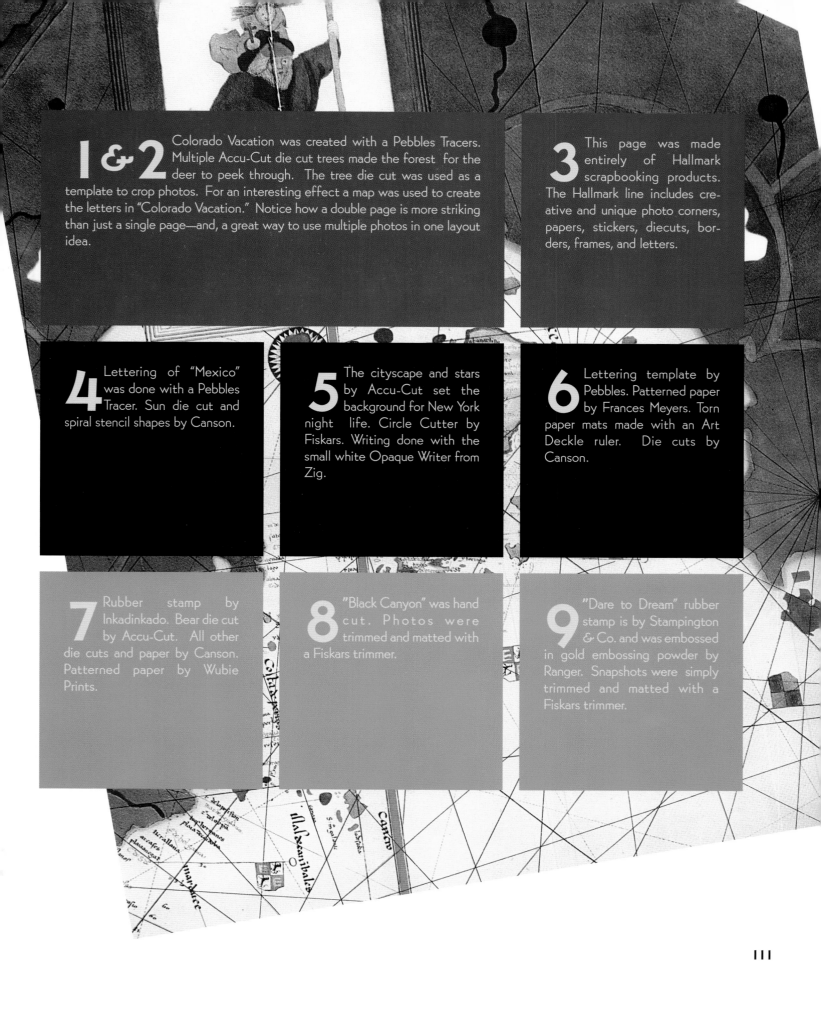

1 & 2 Colorado Vacation was created with a Pebbles Tracers. Multiple Accu-Cut die cut trees made the forest for the deer to peek through. The tree die cut was used as a template to crop photos. For an interesting effect a map was used to create the letters in "Colorado Vacation." Notice how a double page is more striking than just a single page—and, a great way to use multiple photos in one layout idea.

3 This page was made entirely of Hallmark scrapbooking products. The Hallmark line includes creative and unique photo corners, papers, stickers, diecuts, borders, frames, and letters.

4 Lettering of "Mexico" was done with a Pebbles Tracer. Sun die cut and spiral stencil shapes by Canson.

5 The cityscape and stars by Accu-Cut set the background for New York night life. Circle Cutter by Fiskars. Writing done with the small white Opaque Writer from Zig.

6 Lettering template by Pebbles. Patterned paper by Frances Meyers. Torn paper mats made with an Art Deckle ruler. Die cuts by Canson.

7 Rubber stamp by Inkadinkado. Bear die cut by Accu-Cut. All other die cuts and paper by Canson. Patterned paper by Wubie Prints.

8 "Black Canyon" was hand cut. Photos were trimmed and matted with a Fiskars trimmer.

9 "Dare to Dream" rubber stamp is by Stampington & Co. and was embossed in gold embossing powder by Ranger. Snapshots were simply trimmed and matted with a Fiskars trimmer.

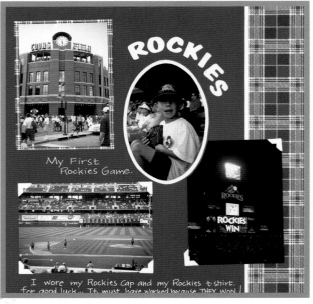

10 Denim paper by Paper Pizazz from H.O.T.P. Footprint stickers and lettering template by Frances Meyers. Pen embellishment created with a Marvy Uchida white gel roller. **11** Jeep and truck paper by Paper Pizazz from H.O.T.P. Boot sticker and lettering template by Frances Meyers. Cooler and lantern stickers by Stickopotamus. Picnic table hand cut from Frances Meyers' wood-grain paper. Photo corners and paper by Canson. **12** Snowflake punch by Family Treasures. "SKI" created with Mrs. Grossman's stickers. Photo corners and paper by Canson. **13** Patterned paper by Paper Patch. Photos trimmed with a Déjà Views template. Photo corners and paper by Canson. "Rockies" lettering was made with Designer Letters by Déjà Views. All other lettering made with an Opaque Writer by Zig.

TIP: Let your children take time to smell the flowers; while they are sniffing, snap their picture!

14 White Water Raft Trip waves were created with a Déjà Views Ruler. Paper by Canson. Sun die cut by Canson. **15** Lettering created with a Pebbles template. Paper by Paper Patch. Photo cut with a Fiskars Circle Cutter. **16** The road border was made with a Déjà Views Ruler. "New York" was hand cut. Just in case you're not able to get all the photos you want, make sure you pick up plenty of postcards to crop and display. Cityscape by Accu-Cut and the apple punched shape by Marvy Uchida. **17** Frames created with Zig pens and a lot of imagination.

14	15
16	17

TIP: To keep your photos and written memories centerstage—lay it out and check it out, before you glue it down.

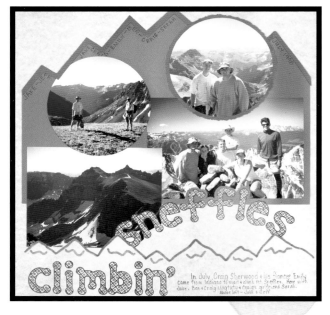

18 All border designs were created with Canson die cuts. "Tucson, Arizona" was spelled out with Inkadinkado's rubber stamps. Double mats for photos trimmed with Fiskar Paper Edgers.   **19** This page was made with Hallmark die cut shapes, stickers and border designs.   **20** When you tell the story of your vacation, use plenty of your own nature and scenery shots mixed with postcards. Stickers by Stickopotamus. Photo mats trimmed with a Fiskars Stamp Paper Edger.   **21** These special photos were trimmed with a Fiskars Circle Cutter. Lettering created with Paper Patch Paper and a Pebbles Tracer.

22 Photos were simply trimmed and matted with hand cut stones tucked around them. "Owl Creek Pass" was hand cut. All paper by Canson. **23** Déjà Views 3-D Keeper stores dimensional memorabilia. Torn paper mats created from Canson paper. Spiral die cuts from Canson. **24** This page was made entirely from Hallmark scrapbooking products. **25** All clip art from D.J. Inkers by Dianne J. Hook. Airplane die cut by Ellison. Fiskar Paper Edgers trimmed the mats and photos.

22	23
24	25

TIP: "Scrapbooking As A Learning Tool" (another TweetyJill publication) is for parents, teachers and homeschoolers who want to do a rewarding scrapbook project with children!

115

26 Matthew and Joel's arrival day at Shamineau's Summer Camp was created with Accu-Cut die cut letters, Paper Patch patterned paper and Stickopotamus stickers. **27** Marvy Uchida punched shapes created the punch art for this page. Photos trimmed with Marvy Uchida Corner Punch. This page was created by Marieda Sawyer for her nieces and nephews (a rehearsal for their airplane trip). **28** Camp Shamineau letters by Pebbles Funky Tracer. Paper by Canson. All pen detail and embellishments by Zig. **29** This cute fishing memories page was cut by hand to feature these special little fishermen! Lettering by Zig.

 TIP: When using stickers, die cuts and patterned papers—know when to stop!

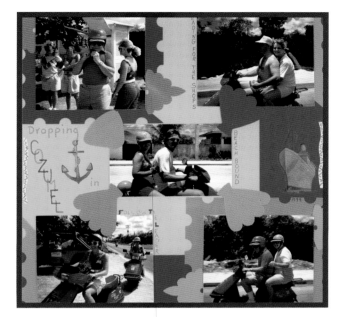

30 Die cuts and paper by Canson showcase these memorable cruise photos taken in Cozumel, Mexico. **31** This pocket page was made using Accu-Cut die cut shapes and paper by Paper Patch and Canson. Put a pocket page in your vacation album to hold all the memorabilia from your trip. A pocket page allows you to look through your keepsakes easily at anytime. **32** Paper by Canson. Die cuts by Accu-Cut. Photo cropped with a Déjà Views template. Snowflake lettering template was used to emboss the background. Lettering by Zig. **33** Die cut shapes and paper by Accu-Cut—sold by Cut-It-Up. Cute page by Vicki Breslin!

30	31
32	33

Memorabilia (mem' ər ə bil' ē ə) n. pl. things worth remembering or recording, as a collection of anecdotes, accounts, memoirs, etc.

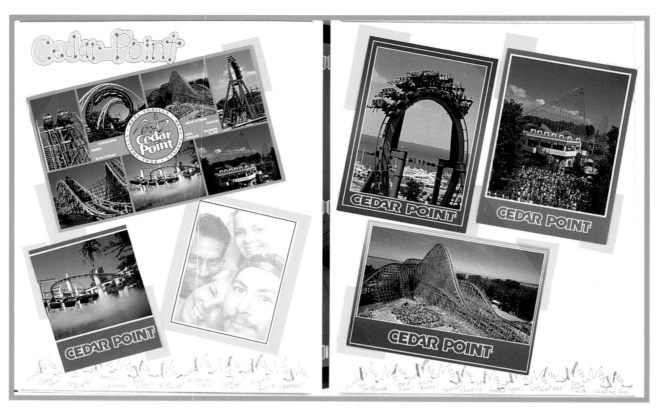

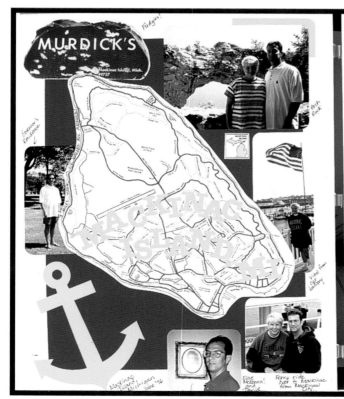

TIP: The memories we document will not only brighten your days, but future generations as well! Think about it.

34 Shari is a lover of roller coasters and collects postcards of all those she has ridden. Artwork was hand-drawn. **35** Shari has created a collage of a vacation with her husband David. Anchor die cuts by Ellison. Photos were trimmed with Uchida's Corner Rounder. **36** "Let's Go Fishing" was created entirely from One Heart, One Mind's multi-use stencils and a stamp pad! Try these stencils for pages with a creative flair. **37&38** Paper and die cut shapes by Canson. Wave design created by tracing and cutting with a Déjà Views Ruler. "Can of Worms" was crimped with a Fiskars Crimper. Notice how the fishing line is drawn out of the photo and connects to the die cut fish. Clever touch!

34	36
35	37 38

TIP: Choose die cut shapes you like and trace them onto your favorite paper, cut out the design for a custom die shape!

Travel Abroad

Stickers on your traveling trunk speak volumes of your journeys. Dancing in the streets of Rio during Carnivale, choosing fresh cut spring flowers at the Paris market, talking to a student for hours on the night train from Warsaw to Prague; the stamps in your passport barely begin to tell your story. Your feet have walked on sand and soil half a world away. You've been a stranger suddenly befriended, and made to feel at home in a foreign land. You've come to realize that people really aren't all that different and a smile is a smile in any language.

Standing in a single shaft of sunlight peeking between cathedral stones, smelling salt air as you cruised out to sea, standing in ruins of the ancients—remember all of it again and again through the curious mementos you collected. It may have been a matchbook, a pebble or panoramic shots of the Eiffel Tower (taken vertically to somehow convey how high it really is when you're looking down)—fragments of each destination serve as uniquely essential reminders of what you saw, who you were with at that moment, and how it made you feel.

Opposite page: Double page layout made with Canson album, photo corners, paper and die cuts. Lettering created with a Funky Tracer by Pebbles. Family Treasures' Deckle and Jumbo Series wave scissors used for mat and border.

Life at Home

A Tismenicja Homestead

Animal Pens and Kitchen Garden

Pets outside! Ivan and a train

Life at Church

St. Nicholas Ukrainian Catholic Church

We arrive in Ukraine!

Wednesday, July 9th

Lviv Airport

1 When you have a lot of assorted pictures from one vacation, and you don't want to crop them, use this simple technique. Make a collage of photos and memorabilia and combine with your journaling. **2&3** A map makes an interesting background for a photo and you can also mark your travel route. Shari went to the Ukraine last year to meet her family, and of course many rolls of film came home with her.

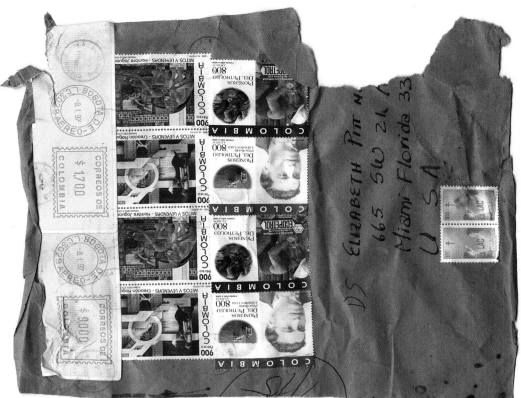

TIP: Use songs, book titles, Bible scriptures, or even TV shows to title your pages. Examples include: A Star is Born, Endless Love, Ain't She Sweet?, On the Road Again, Home Improvement, Touched By an Angel, Wonder Years...etc.

TIP: Search the web for the latest scrapbook news and ideas. Start with Jangle.com.

4 All rubber stamps on this page are from Stampington & Co. and were stamped with Adirondack acid-free ink pads which are available through Ranger. Border was cut with Family Treasures' Antique Elegance, Jumbo Series scissors. Copper embossing powder available through Ranger. Photo corners and papers by Canson. Classic rubber stamps work well with a travel abroad theme. They are an elegant and artistic complement to this type of snapshot. **5** Paper and photo corners by Canson. Suitcase and tag rubber stamp images by Judi-Kins. **6** The sunset was hand cut. Cityscape by Accu-Cut. Photo corners by Canson are a must for European travel photographs! **7 & 8** If you have a few panoramic shots, you may want to showcase them. Tell your special story with choice words and the best photographs and postcards!

WORLD TRAVEL

TIP: Old passport memorabilia can be placed in photo corners to add character to a page.

Kraków

KRAKÓW

KRAKÓW · WAWEL

KRAKÓW

Our hotel was across the Wistula River from Wawel!

Our favorite destination on our entire vacation!

"Dragon "Bones" Wawel's Cathedral

Gorgeous Wawel Gardens The King's Residence.

Kraków WAWEL

KRAKÓW

Wawel Castle

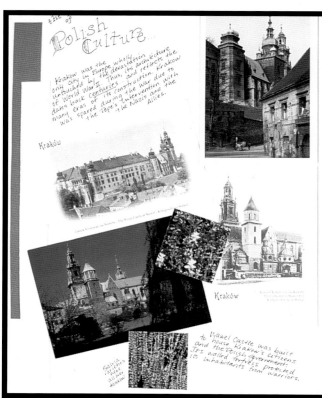

the of
Polish Culture...

Kraków was the only city in Europe wholly untouched by the devastation of World War II. Thus, its architecture dates back centuries, and reflects the many eras of its construction. Kraków was spared during the war due to the Pope's intervention with the Nazis and the Allies.

Kraków

Kraków

Kraków

Wawel Castle was built to house Kraków's citizens and the Polish government. Its walled fortress protected its inhabitants from warriors.

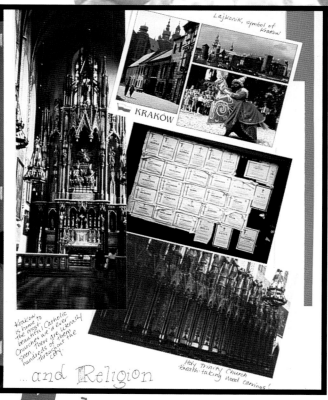

Lajkonik, Symbol of Kraków

KRAKÓW

Kraków is home to the most beautiful Catholic churches we've ever seen. There are literally hundreds of them throughout the city.

Holy Trinity Church breath-taking wood carvings!

...and Religion

Just a little hint of color will enhance your pages tremendously!
TIP:

School

A TEACHER, A FRIEND

A teacher is a person who has the task each day—
Of imparting understanding to each child who comes her way
And making sure her students learn skills of many kinds
Inspiring and encouraging their young, aspiring minds.

With love and guidance she may play a very special part—
In touching very deeply a child's tender heart
For teachers are looked up to by the students that they teach
A special bond begins to grow in each young mind they reach...

Along with academics, there are lessons to instill—
Of just as great importance to the hearts and minds she'll fill
It takes unselfish patience and dedicated care
And maybe even sometimes a special little prayer

She knows that it's her gentle words or smile a child needs
And she's aware that each new day she's planting little seeds—
Of knowledge and encouragement that in each child will grow
Long after the time comes for her to let each child go...

Excerpts from "A Teacher, A Friend," a poem by Linda A. Jones, Treasured Reflections.
Copyright 1997. All rights reserved.

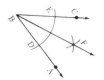

Opposite: Designed using Canson paper and die cut shapes. Lettering created with an Opaque Writer by Zig.

128

TIP: If you want to document a specific year in your album, contact CK Clips at 888-451-8080. They can provide a scrapbook page with all the key events of that year—with room for a photo too!

1 This "Back-to-School" page was created with Canson die cuts and trimmed photos. Take a look at how the adhesive-backed die cuts were pressed onto different colored papers.

2 This is a small variation of the same theme. Press your die cut onto a contrasting color, then trim leaving a margin of color to enhance the design. A Zig Opaque Writer was used for the lettering.

3 Hand-cut letters. Solid paper by Canson. Patterned paper by Paper Patch. Ovals cropped using a Déjà Views template.

4 We all know how important the first day back to school can be. Try taking snapshots to see how your children grow over the years. Heart, flower and school die cuts by Accu-Cut. Cloud die cut by Canson. Designer sticker letters from Déjà Views.

5 Create a school-note pocket page easily with Canson school die cuts and a Déjà Views ruler. "School Notes" was written with a white Zig Opaque Writer. All paper by Canson.

6 Camera, stars and film-strip die cuts are from Canson. This cute page features two cousins on an antique hunting day with grandma.

7 A Déjà Views Ruler created the scalloped border. Paper by Design Originals. Red-dotted paper by Paper Pizazz from H.O.T.P. Design Line stickers by Mrs. Grossman's. Edge border created with Paper Adventures Mammoth Accents Scissors. Layering papers really shows off a special snapshot!

8 To create a blackboard, use black paper and a white Zig Opaque Writer for "chalk." Make a frame for the chalk board with a brown pen. Die cuts by Canson.

9 Patterned paper by Paper Patch. Solid-colored paper by Canson. Stickers by Provo Craft. Designer Letters by Déjà Views.

TIP: If your photos are stored in magnetic albums that are damaging and discoloring them, remove them fast! If they are stuck to the page, use dental floss to gently remove them.

10 Paper, die cuts, frames and stickers by Hallmark. **11** Lettering was formed by Déjà Views Designer Letters. Die cut shapes by Accu-Cut. Punched shape by Marvy Uchida. A Fiskars Paper Edger and Circle Cutter did the trimming. **12** Lettering created with Opaque Writers of various colors by Zig. Stickers by Stickopotamus. Giant "C" created with a Déjà Views lettering template. **13** Letters, die cuts, stickers and numbers by Hallmark. Hallmark has designed frames that work perfectly with your photos. **14** At a Class Reunion you collect dozens of photos! Use a collage layout for groups of snapshots. Combine photos with memorabilia and keepsakes from your events.

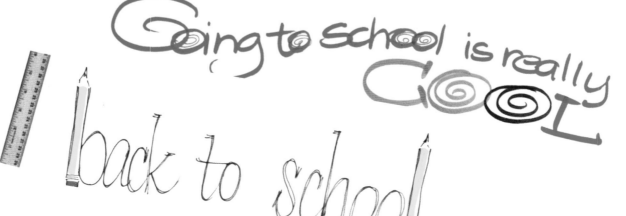

TIP: Scrapbooks are so rewarding; they can build self-esteem, heal hurts, create smiles, and bring laughter and tears. The best part is they last forever! Consider giving one as a gift. Make sure to include a few pages made by you!

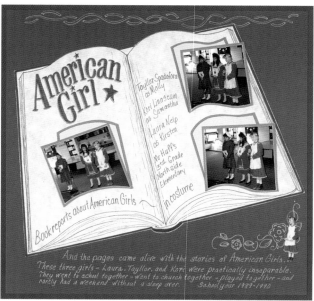

15 16
17 18

15 Make a blackboard and frame with Canson paper and a Zig Opaque Writer. Pencils were hand-drawn. Paper and photo corners by Canson. **16** Pencil and globe were hand-cut. Corners created with a Marvy Uchida Corner Rounder. Make your own mat by cutting a picture into an oval; then, place colored paper beneath it and trim with a Corner Rounder. Creative Letters by Making Memories. Design Line sticker borders by Mrs. Grossman's. **17** "Open book" and "American Girl" letters were hand cut; other lettering created with a Zig Opaque Writer. **18** Pocket pages (for keepsakes) are very easy to make. Here, we used a Marvy Uchida apple Frame Punch to create the top border. Add Canson die cuts and Déjà Views Designer Letters to duplicate this page. A Stickopotamus sticker appears on memorabilia.

A lettering book will help you get the most from all your pen tips.

TIP:

Use a Fiskars perforated blade to create a realistic "quilt-patchwork" paper background.

TIP:

TIP: Trace your child's hand; then, let her use an acid-free stamp pad and her little fingers to add "fingerprints." You may want your child to autograph her school page.

19 The small hand shape was created with a McGill punch. Apple die cut is from Ellison. Trace your child's hand at different ages and use her little fingerprints for a lasting keepsake. Paper by the Paper Company and Paper Patch. Mrs. Grossman's Design Line sticker border. **20** Shari Vu created this page of her "VU Crew" learning retail sales at the S.M.A.R.T. Shop. Stickers by Mrs. Grossman's. Clip art by The S.M.A.R.T. Shop. **21** Die cuts by Accu-Cut. Sprinkle in a few of Mrs. Grossman's musical stickers. Writing done with Zig pens. **22** Sarah's favorite teacher deserves a special place in her album; so, her mom created a memorable page for her! All die cuts and photo corners by Canson. Chalk on the blackboard is really a white Zig Opaque Writer.

| 19 | 20 |
| 21 | 22 |

23 Designs were made with Canson die cuts and Marvy Uchida punched-out stencil shapes. Border made with a Déjà Views Ruler. **24** Jake worked hard that summer! "Jake" letters by Pebbles Tracer. All paper by Canson. Zig Opaque Writer used for lettering. **25&26** "Last Day of High School" page was well worth all the effort it took to make it. After all, how many last days of high school do your children have? Preserve it in a special way! Paper by Wubie Prints. Letters by Pebbles Funky Tracer. Stylized cropping with Déjà Views Templates and Fiskars Paper Edgers.

27 Checkered border by Frances Meyer. Solid-color paper by Canson. Pebbles Tracer used for embossing and lettering. **28** Black checkerboard paper by Frances Meyer. Dotted paper by Paper Patch. "Record" made with a Fiskars Circle Cutter. All lettering was done with a Zig Opaque Writer. **29** Patterned paper by Over The Moon Press. Blue patterned paper by Paperbilities III. A Fiskars Dragonback Paper Edger was used to crop the circular mat. White Opaque Writer by Zig used for journaling. Fiskars Circle Cutter used to crop photo. Photo corners by Canson. **30** Plaid paper by Wubie Prints. Red paper with black stars by Paperbilities III. Silver paper by Paper Pizzaz from H.O.T.P. Metallic gel roller by Marvy Uchida. Photo corner stickers by Frances Meyer. Photo mats cropped with Fiskars Dragonback Paper Edger.

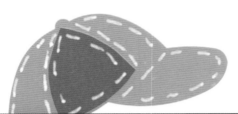

Sports

Remember the first time you threw a baseball like a big kid, swam the whole way across the pool or sunk a real basket from the free throw line? It was serious stuff and it meant you were finally big enough to be included.

Sports teach us life lessons. We learn to conquer defeat with dignity and achieve victory with humility. Playing sports instills respect for competition and our competitors.

We celebrate the athlete because we all understand the challenge of striving to reach a goal; we celebrate the union of training and talent and sheer determination that defines the competitive athlete. We stretch our muscles and our minds and by practicing good sportsmanship, we even touch our hearts. Heroes are found at the Olympics and the Little League field and sometimes even in the stands. Sports motivate and encourage us to push ourselves to be just a little better...to try just a little harder.

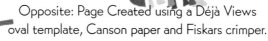

Opposite: Page Created using a Déjà Views
oval template, Canson paper and Fiskars crimper.

When you make a sports page, choose bright action-colors (like blue, orange or yellow).

TIP:

TIP: Try slicing the top or bottom of your photo to show a-c-t-i-o-n!

1 Eric's pictures were laid out like a baseball diamond; the glove snapshot was cropped using a die cut as a template. Die cuts by Accu-Cut.

2 Rubber stamp by Inkadinkado. Stickers by Provo Craft. Paper and photo corners by Canson. Yellow paper by The Paper Company.

3 Die cuts by Canson. Border created with patterned paper from Paper Patch. Lettering created with stickers and imagination!

4 Check out those future football players! Family Treasures Jumbo Series Wave scissors, Canson die cut shapes, and a Marvy Uchida gel roller detailed the die cuts and mat.

5 "Field Day" title designed using Paper Patch paper and a Pebbles template. Photos matted using Fiskars Pinking Paper Edgers. White Zig Opaque Writer used for lettering.

6 Blue Jays page created with Déjà Views Designer Sticker Letters. Photos, baseball and mats cut with a Fiskars Paper Edger. Paper by Canson. Star shape punch by Marvy Uchida .

7 Letters hand cut from a ski resort trail map. Canson paper was torn to make snow-covered mountains. Notice how little skier Lindsay is featured and other photos were cut to fit around her. Try this technique!

8 The Fiskars Crimper was used to give dimension to paper. Fiskars Corner Edgers were used to trim the corners of the photos.

9 Paper by Paper Pizazz from H.O.T.P. Photos cropped with a template by Déjà Views. White lettering by Zig Opaque Writer.

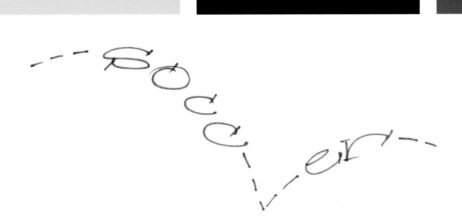

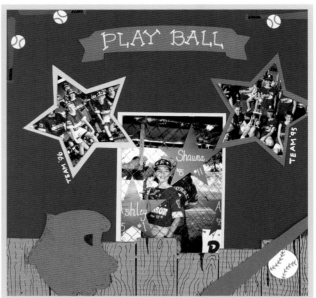

10 11 12 13

10 "Batter Up" was created especially for Joel by Mom. Border formed using a Déjà Views Ruler, Marvy Uchida's circle punch and a Zig Opaque Writer. Mats are torn Canson paper. **11** "Play Ball" created using a Déjà Views Template to crop and mat photos. Accu-Cut die cuts and Stickopotamus baseball stickers enhance this page. A Fiskars Crimper created the fence! **12** This page was designed for Jason. Paper and die cuts by Canson. All Stampington and Co. rubber stamps used on this layout. **13** Entire page made using Fresh-N-Funky Stencils by One Heart-One Mind. Accu-Cut football die cut.

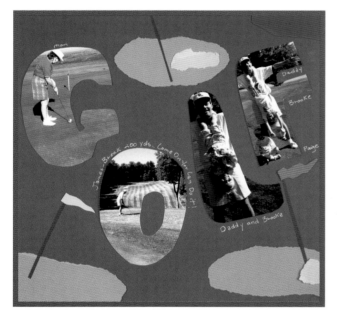

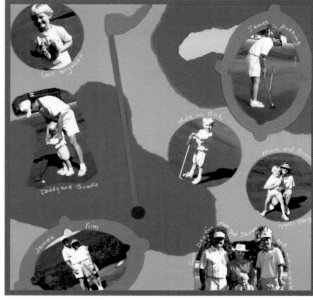

14 Michael is prominently featured in this City Champs photo. Cropping by Déjà Views Templates. Die cuts by Canson. Mats trimmed with Fiskars Paper Edgers. Zig Opaque Writer used for lettering.   15 Canson and The Paper Company paper used on this layout. Kite was hand cut. Photos stacked to create a panoramic look. 16 & 17 The Cornetet family plays golf together. "GOLF" letters hand-cut from photos. Paper by Canson was torn to create the "golf course." Additional pictures were cropped with a Fiskars Circle Cutter and Déjà Views Mix n' Mat. White Zig Opaque Writer used for lettering.

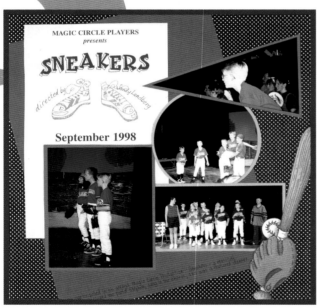

18 | **19**
20 | **21**

18 Lindsay Ostrom's artistic talents! Die cuts by Accu-Cut. Mrs. Grossman's letter stickers were used. **19** Simple page made with uncropped photos. Remember you don't have to crop at all! **20** Sneakers page was created using baseball die cuts and templates by Provo Craft. **21** Little League clip art from D.J. Inkers by Dianne J. Hook. Mrs. Grossman's baseball stickers complete the theme. Die cuts by Ellison.

Jake + Haans on a team in a scrimmage against the CSU Women's Team. The Gang with Fall '97

JAKE DUNKS!

Haans dunks!

Our first game was against the Mavericks. They are a very good team. NOT A GOOD DRAW !!! We lost 45/65. Oh well, we felt like we played our best and that's what counts.

AAU TOURNAMENT March 21, 1998

On the trail

Ridgway, CO.

SOCCER

Jason is 8 yr. old here and loves to play soccer! He joined the Fury team in Sarasota, FL and plays 3 times a week.

Jason

22 "Jake Dunks" was created with Paper Patch basketball paper. The center photo was cut using a Provo Craft circle template. **23** Page designed by Windows of Time. **24** "On the Trail" was created with a Fiskars trimmer, Zig Opaque Writer, and striped paper by Paper Pizazz from H.O.T.P. Notice how the photos are cropped to fit like a puzzle. **25** Soccer and grass die cuts by Accu-Cut. Soccer letters from Making Memories' Creative Letters. Make a dual colored die cut using two soccer balls and cutting and pasting.

22 23
24 25

Memorable Events

A first tooth, first fish, first trophy, first car; all noteworthy triumphs preserved in photographs and heartfelt written memories. These events shape our lives and our destiny. They document our search for what we want to be as we discover who we are. They comprise our fifteen minutes of fame achieved through swimming meets and talent shows, dance recitals and community awards. Milestones are prominent achievements, efforts recognized, dreams realized.

Riding free without training wheels, running for senior class president, renting that first apartment and acquiring those yard sale treasures that gave it charm. Do you remember your challenges and victories? Milestones are personal moments that help define us. These memories instantly invoke a feeling of accomplishment, a satisfied, private reflection.

Opposite: Page designed using Accu-Cut die cuts and a Déjà Views ruler. Album and solid color paper by Canson. Patterned paper by Paper Patch. White Zig Opaque Writer used for lettering.

The Original Scrapbook Convention

SUMMIT
Ministries

In August '98 Laura spent two weeks in Manitou Springs at Summit – an intense study of the Christian world view – increasing her faith & making great friends. It really was life changing & awesome!

Jayce · Gracy · Laura · Amber · Shannon · Laurel

Mariel   Katie   Laura

DREAM

HOME

Matts Graduation – Air Force Academy
May 27, 1998

Voice Recital

Laura sang a duet with Martha Caulfield, a duet with Hannah Gilham, and a solo. Debbie Turner – instructor.   MAY 1998

My First Haircut

Before...

...After

Aunt Prissy fixed your hair like this?, so I decided it was time for your first haircut. The barber gave you a lollipop to keep you

Laura was a poster contest winner – got to meet Smokey the Bear – got to ride on a float – and got a "Smokey's Helper" tee shirt.

International Scrapbook Trade
Education ❧ Inspiration ❧ Preservation

1	2	3
4	5	6
7	8	9

1 Capture special times using Paper Patch paper to create a pennant. Use Fiskars Paper Edgers to trim mats.

2 Sarah's raft trip was such a memorable event for her. This bright-colored page enhances the photos well and was simply done with a Déjà Views Ruler and Accu-Cut paddle die cut.

3 Design created by Lindsay Ostrom and Vicky Breslin with their Rule-It-Up Rulers by Cut-It-Up. Rule-It-Up Rulers are a versatile stencil and ruler all in one. Collect the whole set to have endless creativity at hand!

4 Record your teen's ministry events to pass down to future generations. These pages will show their priorities at that tender time of growing and changing. Paper Patch paper, Fiskars Paper Edgers and Circle Cutter. Writing created with Pebbles Tracers and a Zig Opaque Writer.

5 Light blue check paper by Paperbilities III from MPR and Associates. Frances Meyers stickers. Blue print by Paper Pizazz from H.O.T.P. Lettering created with a Pebbles Tracer. Mats for photos made with Marvy Uchida's Corner Rounder and Fiskars Paper Edgers.

6 Canson's red, white and blue paper and Accu-Cut die cut stars give this patriotic page eye appeal! White stripes were hand cut.

7 Paper by Geographics. Mats trimmed by Fiskars Paper Edgers. Circular photo cut with Fiskars Circle Cutter.

8 Stickers are by Provo Craft. The barbershop pole was hand designed by Lori Pieper. Fiskars Corkscrew Paper Edgers and Déjà Views Templates enhance the snapshots from that special day when Johnny first lost his curls.

9 Solid-colored paper and die cut shapes by Canson. Patterned paper by Paper Patch. Corner border by Zig Opaque Writer. Balloons cut with a Fiskars Circle Cutter.

10 Use favorite cards or part of the event announcement, as a mat. Remember to back the photo with acid-free paper first. Photo cropped with Déjà Views Template. Lettering done with Zig acid-free pens. Paper by Canson. **11** Paper for "three little monkeys" by Provo Craft. Hand-cut letters. Snapshots trimmed with a Marvy Uchida Corner Rounder. **12** Paper embossing done with a Pebbles template. White Zig Opaque Writer used for lettering. Fiskars Paper Edgers used to trim mat. **13** Paper and die cuts by Canson. Lettering created with a Pebbles Tracer.

14 The weird hair day was created with hand-cut paper shapes and Canson die cuts. Accu-Cut scrapbook letters were used for the title. 15 Paper by Canson. Lettering done with a Zig Opaque Writer. Keep track of your teen's special events and try to keep up with your pages, and you will have a great graduation gift someday! 16 The Albuquerque Zoo page has a southwestern border die cut from Canson. Cropping was done with a Déjà Views template and Fiskars Scallop Scissors. Creative lettering was done with a Zig Opaque Writer.

14 15
16

THE GRADUATE

TIP: Let your child document a page for you once in a while. Encourage them with reminders of the event to prompt their writing.

ZOO

Eric and Joel watching the panther

BUSCH GARDENS

Busch Gardens

Joel, Sarah and Eric visit the Sanford, Florida Zoo - Jan. 1995

A doe and fawn

YMCA

SHARKS

My first swim meet - Venice, Florida Summer of '94

NATIONAL YMCA MEET

Sharks have plenty of individual stars

By Phil Moran

I can't believe it! I won!

official Time

LINDSAY HAGLUND

EVENT: 25 Back

TIME OR BEST TIME: 25.88

COMMENTS: Great Job!

Super! #1 Winner!

I had butterflies in my stomach all the way to the meet. The pool was HUGE — it was Olympic size! Jason, Matthew, Mom, and Dad all came to watch. I could hear them cheering for me while I was swimming the freestyle!

17 18 | 21
19 20 | 22

15A

TIP: Make sure you copy newspaper articles on acid-free paper before adding them into your scrapbook. They will last indefinitely without yellowing.

TIP: If you're at a loss for words when you begin to document, just look at a photograph of the person, event or place—think back to the time you were there—then start to write what comes to mind.

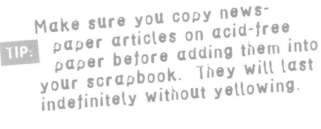

17&18 This page created with paper by Canson and Fiskars Paper Edgers. Family Treasures' Jumbo Series Scallop scissors cut giraffe's mane. 19&20 Lindsay's swim meet will be forever remembered, thanks to a page created especially for her. Shark die cut by Accu-Cut and award pennant by Canson. Lettering by Zig Opaque Writer. 21 This page was made entirely of Hallmark scrapbooking products. The Hallmark line includes creative and unique photo frames, designed papers, stickers and borders. 22 This adorable Zoo page was created with a Paper Piecing Pattern and Critter paper by Windows of Time. Add pen stitches for die cut embellishment!

Je t'aime

152

Wedding

He's your best friend, your companion, your biggest fan; your husband. You are building a life together. Whether you recited vows five years ago or fifty, it seems like yesterday when you glance at those photos. You relive those heart-pounding moments when you exchanged infinite promises before God and family and began a life-long journey together.

Every time you brush your hand across the parchment paper the memories touch your heart. There is something old; an antique lace applique that adorned your gown. Something new is there as well; the velvet-smooth silk ribbon that cascaded from your veil, something borrowed; a penny from your maid of honor, never requiring repayment, and something blue; the solitary blue forget-me-not that stood humbly amongst a sea of white roses in a bouquet now pressed and preserved. So many memories flood your heart to have and to hold from this day forward.

Opposite: Albums by Kolo. Paper and die cuts by Canson. "Love" is Accu-Cut letters. Fiskars Paper Edgers and Circle Cutter cropped mats. Dream Weaver Brass Stencil created heart embossing. "I believe in miracles" stamp on Canson's hand shape die cut from D.J. Inkers by Diane J. Hook.

1 2
3 4

1 & 2 Dean and Terry Burnside's double-page wedding layout was made entirely from Canson products. Canson has a full line of albums, die cuts, photo corners, paper and adhesives for scrapbooking. The corner treatments were designed using a Fiskars Rotary Cutter. Fiskars Ripple Paper Edgers were used on the white mats for photos. **3** Die cuts are from Canson's wedding pack. Small embossed foil flying bird is from Stampington & Co. **4** Cuts were made with a Rotary Cutter and Ripple Paper Edger from Fiskars. Canson's wedding die cuts were used to enhance the photographs.

5 A collage was created with a clip art border and small squares of color which frame the important memorabilia and photographs. Clip art is from D. J. Inkers by Diane J. Hook. **6** Paper by Canson. Corner treatments designed with a Corner Lace Punch by Family Treasures. Borders created with a border punch by Family Treasures. **7** This page is made entirely with Hallmark scrapbooking products.

A Stamp In Hand® (310) 329-8555 rubber stamps

Accu-Cut Systems® (800) 288-1670 *Accu-Cut Roller System*™ die cut machines, dies, papers and more. Die cuts sold by Crafty Cutter® (805) 237-7833 and Cut-It-Up® (530) 389-2233

All Night Media Rubber Stamps® (415) 459-0606, (800) 326-4226 rubber stamps

CK Clips® (941) 747-0070 *"Seems Like Yesterday"*™ cardstock pages featuring happenings from years past.

C-Thru Ruler Company® (860) 243-0303 *see Déjà Views*

Canson® (413) 538-9250 albums, paper, self-adhesive paper, die cuts and photo corners

Chatterbox®, Inc. (888)272-3010 *Journaling Genie*™

Clearsnap®, Inc. (360) 293-6634 *Top Boss*™ embossing pad, *Colorbox Ink*™ pads and *Rollagraph Roller Stamp System*™ and rubber stamps

Colorbök® (wholesale only) (734) 426-5300 die cuts and scrapbook supplies

Commotion® *The Art of Rubber Stamping*™ (520) 746-0515 rubber stamps

Crafty Cutter® (805) 237-7883 Accu-Cut, Ellison and Crafty Cutter exclusive line die cuts.

Creative Card Company® (312) 666-8686 papers

Cut-It-Up® (530) 389-2233 *Rule-It-Up*™ rulers and books: "Clip-It-Up", "Rule-It-Up", "Rule-It-Up, Two," "Creative Doodles", and Lindsay Ostrom's "L,M,N,O,P and More Creative Lettering by Lindsay," die cuts and papers

Déjà Views (860) 243-0303 *Déjà Views Viewler*™, *Déjà Views Doodads*™, *Déjà Views Spot Lettering Templates*™, *Déjà Views Mix n' Mat Template*™, *Déjà Views Acid-Free Designer Letters*™

Delta® (562) 695-7969 *Delta Cherished Memories*™ stencils

Denami Design® (253) 639-2546 rubber stamps

Design A Card® (941)475-1121 *The Art Deckle ruler*™

Design Originals® 800-877-7820 *Scrap Happy*™ Acid-Free Paper - Girls, Keepsake and Vintage series

DJ Inkers® (800) 944-4680 rubber stamps and clip art by Dianne J. Hook

DreamWeaver® Stencils (909) 824-8343 Brass embossing templates

EK Success® LTD (800) 524-1349 *Zig Opaque Writer*™ acid-free pens, *Memory Series*™ colored pencils, *Stickopotamus Stickers*™, and *Tracers*™

Ellison® (888) 253 2238 die cut *Lettering Machine*™, dies and more

Family Treasures® (800) 413-2645 *Corner Slot*™ punch, *Jumbo Series*™ scissors, *Punchline*™ punches, as well as other punches, rulers and a variety of scrapbook supplies

Fiskars® (715) 842-2091 *Paper Edgers*™, *Corner Edgers*™, *Circle Cutter*™, *Crimper*™, mats, craft knives, portable trimmer and a variety of scrapbook supplies

Frances Meyer®, Inc. (800) 373-6237 Stickers, papers and scrapbook supplies

Fred B. Mullet Stamps® *Stamps from Nature Prints*™ 2707 59th SW, Suite A, Seattle, WA 98116 catalog $4 (refundable), rubber stamps featuring prints from fish, plants and nature

Geographics® (888) 854-7239 paper

Hallmark® Cards, Inc. To find a store near you, go to www.hallmark.com *Frames & Shapes*™, *Journal Stickers*™, *Stickers-Autocollants*™, *Scrapbooking Kids*™, *Border Stickers*™, albums, paper and templates

Hampton Art Stamps® (516) 924-1335 rubber stamps

Hand & Heart® Rubber Stamps, contact Yvonne Perez at HANDHRT@aol.com

Heritage Handcrafts® (303) 683-0963 brass embossing templates

Hero Arts Rubber Stamps® (800) 822-4376

Hot Off The Press®, Inc. (530) 266-9102 *Paper Pizazz*™ printed papers

Inkadinkado Rubber Stamps® (800) 888-4652 rubber stamps

ISTA International Scrapbook Trade Association publishes an educational newspaper for the scrapbook industry (for the consumer and trade). To subscribe call: (972) 318-0491

JANGLE.com is a web site serving the scrapbook enthusiast. News, products, tips, contests and more

Judi-Kins® Rubber Stamps (310) 515-1115 rubber stamps

K & Company® (913) 685-1458 embossed scrapbook pages

Keeping Memories Alive® (800) 419-4949 Papers, die cuts, stickers and scrapbook supplies

Kolo®, Inc. (860) 547-0367 *Newport Photo Albums*,™ *Accordian Albums*™, *Vineyard Mini-Albums*™, *Retro Photo Album*™, *Photo Cards*™

Lasting Impressions for Paper®, Inc (801) 298-1979 brass embossing templates

Magenta Art Stamps® 351 Blain, Mont-Saint-Hilaire, QC, Canada J3H 3B4 rubber stamps

Making Memories® (800) 286-5263 *Creative Letters*™

Mara-Mi® (800) 279-8787 papers

Marshall Company® (847) 821-0450 *Marshall's Photo Coloring System*™ for black and white photos. Plus videos, oil tubes and pencils

McGill®, Inc. (815) 568-7244 punches

Me & My Big Ideas® (949) 589-4607 stickers

Melissa Neufeld®, Inc. (800) 638-3353 stickers

Memories Forever® (877) 375-3316 papers

Memories In Minutes® (702) 456-6661 *Scrapbook Specialties*™, mini-scrapbook kits

Michel & Company® (310) 390-7655 *The Gifted Line*™ stickers

MPR and Associates® retail (800) 454-3331, wholesale (800) 334-1047 *Paperbilities III*™ paper

Mrs. Grossman's Paper Company® (800) 429-4549 decorative stickers and accessories

NRN Designs® (800) 421-6958 papers, stickers and scrapbook supplies

Northern Spy® (530) 620-7430

One Heart, One Mind® LLC (913) 498-3690 *Multi-use Fresh & Funky*™ stencils

Over the Moon Press® (801) 253-9482 papers

Paper Adventures® (414) 383-0414 *Mammoth Edge Accents Scissors*™ and other scrapbooking products.

Papers by Catherine® (713) 723-3334 Beautiful papers, cards, accordian books and more.

Paper Patch® paper (801) 253-3018

Pebbles in My Pocket® (800) 438-8153 *Tracers,* die cuts and more

Personal Stamp Exchange Rubber Stamps® (707) 588-8058, 360 Sutton Place, Santa Rosa, CA 95407 Rubber stamps, embossing powders, ink pads and more.

Posh Impressions® (800) 421-7674 rubber stamps

Provo Craft® (800) 937-7686 *Designer Stickey Die Cuts*™, templates, stickers

Quick Cuts® (714) 671-9438 *Puzzlemate*™ template

Ranger Industries® (732) 389-3535 Acid-free ink pads. *Archival Ink*™, *Adirondack Ink*™, *Big and Juicy*™ ink pads, *Colorit*™, *Gilding Pad*™, *Colorit Pigment Pads*™, embossing powders, brayers and more.

Rubber Stampede® (800) 632-8386 Rubber stamps, ink pads, stamp kits and more

Scrapbook Specialties® *Memories in Minutes*™ Templates for miniature scrapbooks

Stickopotamus® (800) 524-1349 stickers

Stampington & Company® (949) 380-7318 rubber stamps and accessories, boxes, foils and more.

Sonlight Impressions® (909) 278-5656 rubber stamps

Straightforward Stamps® by Judy Pruitt (303) 766-0536

The Ehlers Company, Inc.Imports® (310) 530-2940 Acid-free doilies, gold embossed foils, and more.

The Gift Wrap Company® (912) 884-9727 tissue papers

The Paper Company® (800) 426-8989 papers

The Paper Patch Company® (801) 253-3019 patterned papers

Toy Box Rubber Stamps® (707) 431-1400

Treasured Reflections® Poetry by Linda A. Jones (800) 549-4205 original poetry and verses (including custom poems)

Tsukineko®, Inc. (800) 769-6633 *Dauber Duos*™, *Encore*™ stamp pads and more

Uchida of America® (800) 541-5877 *Marvy Markers*™, *Metallic Gel Rollers*™, *Brites*™, punches and more.

Uptown Rubber Stamps® (800) 888-3212 rubber stamps

Wasatch Mountain Design® (801) 969-1808 Sandy Tyson's "Alphabet Soup" series: books for creative lettering

What's New® Ltd. (620) 830-4581 *Scrap-Ease*™ die cuts

Wildlife Enterprises® (530) 626-5924 rubber stamps

Windows of Time® (801) 732-1053 *Paper Piecing Patterns*™ and books

Wubie Prints® (wholesale only) (801) 256-0185 patterned papers

COLLAGE CREDITS
& Copyright Page

A very special thanks to the following companies that helped make our book beautiful. We deeply appreciate your letting us use your rubber stamps, papers and stickers in this fashion: